Praise for *Small Stories, Big C*

Small Stories, Big Changes left me dazed, inspired and awestruck. The amazing environmental activists featured in Estill's latest book are simply remarkable in their breadth of experience, accomplishments and tenacious persistence in the face of harsh realities and obstacles. Their personal journeys left me with renewed faith that we can still conquer the most difficult and vexing ills that plague our planet.

—Larry Shirley, Director of Operations and Planning for the
Nicholas Institute for Environmental Policy Solutions at Duke University

In Small Stories, Big Changes, editor Lyle Estill introduces us to collection of well-known and unknown amazing people in the throes of doing the work that needs to be done in both small and big ways. Some are Estill's biological family and others are what you could call his biofuel family but they all share the same DNA in their personal and inspiring stories to preserve the earth.

—Paul Cuadros, author, *A Home on the Field,
How One Championship Team Inspires Hope for Small Town America*

This book brings together diverse efforts toward renewal. Lyle has set aside his considerable voice and has conveyed new voices from the growing grassroots movement. *Small Stories, Big Changes* reveals the hard and rewarding work of rejuvenation.

—Jeff Barney, philosopher, owner, Saxapahaw General Store

Lyle Estill is not only a delightfully, engaging writer but a daring maverick in the field of sustainability.

In his first book, *Biodiesel Power*, he made the world of bio-fuels fascinating — even to those of us who had barely heard of the stuff.

Then in *Small is Possible*, Estill introduced us to a magical, yet real community where a marvelous menagerie of people had figured out how to make a "living for one." People are still clambering to get their copy.

In his third book, *Industrial Evolution*, Estill laid out the yellow brick road to carbon neutrality, with tales of Local Food Fridays, Solar Double Cropping, and even being "In Bed With Government."

For his newest book, *Small Stories, Big Changes: Agents of Change on the Frontlines of Sustainability*, Estill chooses to share the baton with a select group of sustainability pioneers and the result is not only compelling and heartwarming, but historic and revolutionary. We owe Estill a huge debt for bringing them to us — so that their stories can inspire us all to take more action, NOW, to make the big changes we *all* have the innate potential to make.

Catching their stories in their own words, combined with his engaging commentary, is a stroke of genius.

For followers of Estill's climb to the summit of the "Green Energy Alps," that comes as no surprise.

—Carol Hewitt, author, *Financing Our Foodshed;*
Growing Local Food With Slow Money

Lyle Estill is a master spinner. His ability to evoke, provoke, delight and draw has long fascinated me. I eagerly read each of his earlier books, allowing his characteristically smart, free-flowing and conversational text to come into my own head-space like a favored party guest. And like that certain guest without whom your party would slip into the "should have gone somewhere else" category, Lyle has yet to disappoint.

I am delighted to find him in a new role with this latest work, as the designated driver, if you will, delivering the words and works of others in our wider community as celebrants, as the favored guests. Each chapter is another introduction, another individual whom we did not expect to find, but without whom we could not imagine the evening continuing.

We should all, in reading this excellent series of accounts, come away with a bit of a buzz, maybe even a headache the next day. These are the folks you simply have to meet. And as it is exceedingly unlikely they will all ever be in the same room at the same time, I have to thank Lyle for introducing us to them in this fashion. Great party. I cannot wait for the next one.

—Geoffrey Neal, poet, spoken word activist

SMALL STORIES
BIG
CHANGES

AGENTS OF CHANGE ON THE
FRONTLINES OF SUSTAINABILITY

LYLE ESTILL

new society
PUBLISHERS

Cover design by Diane McIntosh.
Cover: © iStock (maxphotography); inset: © iStock (CribbVisuals)

Printed in Canada. First printing April 2013.

Paperback ISBN: 978-0-86571-738-1
eISBN: 978-1-55092-533-3

Inquiries regarding requests to reprint all or part of *Small Stories Big Changes*
should be addressed to New Society Publishers at the address below.

To order directly from the publishers, please call toll-free
(North America) 1-800-567-6772, or order online at www.newsociety.com

Any other inquiries can be directed by mail to:

New Society Publishers
P.O. Box 189, Gabriola Island, BC V0R 1X0, Canada
(250) 247-9737

LIBRARY AND ARCHIVES CANADA CATALOGUING IN PUBLICATION

Small stories big changes : agents of change on the frontlines
of sustainability / [edited by] Lyle Estill.

ISBN 978-0-86571-738-1

1. Environmental protection—Citizen participation—Case studies.
2. Environmentalism—Case studies.   3. Sustainable living—Case studies.
I. Estill, Lyle

TD171.7.S63 2013   363.7'0525   C2013-901726-7

New Society Publishers' mission is to publish books that contribute in fundamental ways to building an ecologically sustainable and just society, and to do so with the least possible impact on the environment, in a manner that models this vision. We are committed to doing this not just through education, but through action. The interior pages of our bound books are printed on Forest Stewardship Council®-registered acid-free paper that is 100% post-consumer recycled (100% old growth forest-free), processed chlorine free, and printed with vegetable-based, low-VOC inks, with covers produced using FSC®-registered stock. New Society also works to reduce its carbon footprint, and purchases carbon offsets based on an annual audit to ensure a carbon neutral footprint. For further information, or to browse our full list of books and purchase securely, visit our website at: www.newsociety.com

MIX
Paper from
responsible sources
FSC
www.fsc.org
FSC® C016245

Contents

Also by Lyle Estill

Biodiesel Power:
The Passion, the People and
the Politics of the Next Renewable Fuel

Small is Possible:
Life in a Local Economy

Industrial Evolution:
Local Solutions for a Low Carbon Future

To Ann and Don,
who raised me and my brothers
with permission to change the world.

Foreword

By David W. Orr

The mighty oak tree begins its long life in the forest as an acorn. Mammals began their evolution as tiny creatures at the feet of the dinosaurs. The modern Civil Rights movement started in Rosa Parks' refusal to move from her seat. And even you and I began life as the smallest of infinitesimally small possibilities. Mostly large things grow from the small, very fragile, and the very unlikely, the sort no smart gambler would bet on. But smart gamblers and long odds don't rule the world. Something else is going on.

The smart odds-makers overlook the exquisite set of instructions embedded in a tiny bundle of information wrapped inside a hard-shell acorn that grows a two-hundred-fifty ton, two hundred foot tall, exquisitely beautiful tree that knows how to make more acorns. Evolution, too, has its own logic that we dimly understand, but it favors the agile, the adaptable, and smart over the complacent, powerful, and stupid. Social movements, too, begin in the small acorn of indignation in the offense that finally breaks through hard shell of callous indifference, stony hearts, and oppression. Human possibilities, similarly, start in child-hood fascinations and convictions nurtured by those wise and caring enough to see large potentials in small packages.

The equation by which the possible becoming the actual is rather like the quadratic equations we once solved in math classes; you have to get each part right to arrive at the correct answer. The parts in this case include the core idea, which is the easier part, combined with the spirit which is the force behind the idea, plus the help of a few believers, supporters, and friends who light the way through dark nights, and last the is the stubborn refusal to take "no" for an answer. And then there is mystery that no one understands—the emer-gent properties that come into play when the Universe turns in one's favor. Water, D. H. Lawrence once said is "two parts hydrogen and one part oxygen. But there is a third thing that makes it water and no one knows what it is." In the stories told below there is mystery too, the emergent property and the inexplicable results.

Lyle Estill, an entrepreneur, a doer, a writer, and bridge builder, has collected stories of the small possibilities that are growing into larger realities, movements, and victo-ries ahead. Few would bet much on any one of them, but together they are parts of a larger pattern of change now sweeping across the world. The persons and projects de-scribed below are agile, adaptable, and smart and the Uni-verse is on their side as it once was with small mammals, the oak, the cause of justice, and of Life as well. If you have to gamble (or better, invest), bet on these folks and the millions more like them now shaping a sunshine powered and decent world, not on the dinosaurs, the merchants of carbon, the extractors, the exploiters, and the takers. You won't lose and your descendents will win big.

　—David W. Orr

David Orr is Paul Sears Distinguished Professor and Senior Adviser to the President, Oberlin College. He is the author of seven books including Down to the Wire: Confronting Climate Collapse *and* Hope is an Imperative: The Essential David Orr.

Introduction

I never set out to create or inspire societal change. When it came to renewable energy, I just sort of lumbered along, stepping into one curiosity after another. If anything, I merely had too much time on my hands. My friend Michael Tiemann attributes that in part to my lack of a television set. To hear him tell it I was just a guy with five gallons of turkey fat who wanted to figure out how to make it burn.

He's partly right about that. I might argue that I was more interested in motive power than simple combustion—but close enough is good enough.

My deep frying of turkeys did lead to the creation of biodiesel from used cooking oil, and the creation of biodiesel did lead to the formation of Piedmont Biofuels, and Piedmont Biofuels did go on to become a national pioneer in grassroots community scale biodiesel. That's all true.

What is also true is that I went on to meet an astonishing array of powerful people. I don't count the White House advisors, or Senators, or the sea of politicians that have visited or tapped our project. What inspires me is those individuals who are on the ground, delivering good work in the name of environmental sustainability. They are the voices in this book.

Some of them are well known, with books, essays and articles to their credit. Some of them are family. Some are making their publishing debut. All of their stories are fascinating, and I am delighted to have collected them here.

This book accidentally began with a piece I wrote for my daughter. She was editing a newsletter on renewable energy and I submitted an essay entitled "Agents of Change."

"Change" is a big space. This book is limited to change agents on the environmental and sustainability front. I intentionally left out those people I know who are on the front lines of fighting sexism, racism, corporatism, poverty, hunger and many other good battles.

And I understand how flawed that is. My brother Glen once invited me to a conversation with David Suzuki, and he distilled everything down to hunger and poverty. Suzuki said, "If I was starving, and I saw an animal I could eat, I wouldn't check some list to see if it was endangered. I'd kill it and eat it. That's what I would do."

I think he is right about that. But to assemble a book I needed some criteria—some sort of theme I could stick with—so I chose people with experience in the sustainability field, which left out many dear friends and wonderful writers.

I have happily omitted the point of view of anarchists, greenwashers, talkavists, posers, freeloaders and sustainability consultants who hang out around the sustainability movement. This book is by those people who are actually doing the work that needs to be done.

These are simply stories. Some about flops. Some about successes. Some about ideas that have long since died on the vine. Despite what I might write, or talk about, my own story seems inexorably tied to biodiesel. I intentionally limited the number of biodiesel activists in this book for that reason.

Sometimes I feel trapped in a biodiesel ghetto. And while it is easy for me to resent that, it is through biodiesel that I discovered my own activism. And our unending desire to fuel our community is what has introduced me to the remarkable collection of writers and activists that have made this book possible.

The message of this book is that you are not alone in your fight to effect positive change. I've been inspired by the work of these people, and I am hoping their stories will also inspire you.

Bryan Welch

I met Bryan Welch in the early summer of 2011 at his Mother Earth News Fair in Puyallup, Washington. I had never met him; all I knew was that he was the publisher of a stack of magazines, including *Mother Earth News*, the presenter of the Fair...

I was awestruck by the Fair. I wandered through exhibits of inventions, paused at various demonstrations and was astonished by the throngs of people who were hungry for any ideas that would increase their self-reliance or the resilience of their community. I was there to speak about my book *Industrial Evolution*, but I rapidly found myself more of a consumer than an expert.

Because Bryan was the sponsor of the fair, I felt like his guest, so I found my way to the main stage to hear him speak. I had low expectations. I thought, "He's a magazine magnate throwing a conference. Of course he has center stage."

He walked out in front of a packed audience and instead of taking the podium; he just sort of leaned against it. He was casual, completely relaxed and at home. The audience immediately felt as if they were in good hands and my small-minded suspicion dissolved instantly.

Without any notes he explained how he raises livestock in Kansas. He spoke of his dependence on the prairie and of how he is actually more of a grass farmer than anything else. To my amazement he launched into a discussion of over-population and the carrying capacity of the planet.

After his talk I wanted to meet him, but fans swarmed him. I overheard one middle-aged woman say, "I've been reading Mother Earth News since I was ten years old…"

Here's the story of his journey, from a hardscrabble patch of desert to a magazine empire that feeds the minds of millions of readers…

MOTHER EARTH NEWS

by Bryan Welch

My mentor was a sunburned, 60-year-old, 300-pound Jehovah's Witness in dark glasses. Tim Posey didn't look like a
tree-hugger. He didn't talk about loving nature or saving the
environment. But he was, in many ways, the truest and best
conservationist I've ever known.

I grew up in an enclave of surplus army barracks and mobile homes on the Mexican border a few miles from El Paso,
Texas. Technically we lived in the village of Anapra, in
southern New Mexico. But our community—and our culture—didn't really belong in any either state, or either country. In many ways, the border is its own nation. It's a country
that attracts self-reliant misfits, independent thinkers and
many people who are simply stranded on the margins of the
North American economy.

Mr. Posey bought 10 acres in that economic—and lit-
eral—desert in the 1950s. He drilled a well and buried a network of shallow water lines, dividing the land into a grid of
lots where renters could park their trailers (which have since
come to be called mobile homes). He dug simple septic tanks
with standpipes rising out of the sand. He planted poles and

strung power lines. If you rented a lot in the Posey Trailer Park you could pull your trailer in, hook up the sewer, electricity and water and within an hour or so be ready to settle in and watch *Gunsmoke* on TV.

The great thing about owning a trailer park, Mr. Posey would tell me, was that once you had the water, sewer and power set up, you could pretty much "set back and collect the rent." But Mr. Posey didn't rest on his laurels. Once the trailer park was operational, Tim Posey built himself an oasis.

The Posey homestead probably wouldn't strike most Americans as a vision of paradise. We lived on dunes dotted with creosote and mesquite bushes, cactus and yucca. Mostly, the land was bare sand. We had seven or eight inches of total precipitation a year, which as my Dad liked to say didn't seem like much unless you were there the day it rained seven inches—usually in a single deluge in late June or early July.

Tim Posey had a half-acre vegetable garden irrigated with well water; a collection of sheds and barns built from scavenged poles and plywood; pens for his goats, chickens, geese and ducks; two long rows of rabbit hutches; and a few paddocks and stalls he rented to horse owners.

I started hanging around when I was about 8 years old because I loved animals. By the time I was 9 Tim Posey had hired me to milk the goats, and to take them out to the desert to browse. He said he figured he couldn't get rid of me so he might as well put me to work. I was paid in eggs and milk.

The desert is a goat's natural habitat. Where we see a wasteland of scrubby plants they see a smorgasbord. I would open the gate and watch Tim's little herd of half a dozen dairy goats charge into the scrubland, greedily seeking out their favorites—bunch grass, mesquite beans and purslane. They seemed to enjoy variety. They moved from one species to the next: Seed pods for breakfast, grass for brunch, a big meal of flowering purslane and then maybe a leisurely hour or two munching on mesquite leaves. In the evening we went back to the barn and I witnessed the daily miracle. From the desert's sparse, coarse, resinous plants the goats made sweet, frothy milk loaded with butterfat.

Mr. Posey performed a similar miracle in his garden.

We mixed manure from the pens in a 55-gallon drum with well water, and then poured the slurry into the stream of irrigation water, which carried nourishment to every corner of the plot. Because Mr. Posey had a bad back, it was my job to stir the slurry. If you've ever stuck your head in a barrel full of liquefied chicken manure on a 95-degree afternoon you can confirm that the sensation is less a smell than it is a state of being, like snorkeling in a pond that is equal parts feces and ammonia. Still, it was our magic potion.

There in the heart of the Chihuahuan desert surrounded by sand dunes, Tim Posey cultivated squash and cucumbers, fat watermelons and tall stands of corn. He grew spices and beans, okra and peas.

The desert summer days were long and sunny. The sand was clean and well drained. We added water and fertilizer and, voila, the desert made food. It struck me then, and still seems to me now, a sort of miracle, or at least evidence of a sort of earthy magic, the transubstantiation of sand into watermelons.

The Jehovah's Witnesses encourage their members to create their own food and to protect the planet by using organic methods. But I didn't know, then, that the Posey homestead was inspired by a religion. I only knew that it amazed me and that I felt closer to God there, among the plants and animals that provided our food, than I ever had in a church. I never considered joining the Witnesses, but I guess I became a sort of lower-case witness myself, a witness to the wonder and satisfaction of growing food on a personal scale. And my goat herding evolved, in a roundabout way, into my career.

Since my company acquired it in 2001, *Mother Earth News* has formed the main part of our business, the primary engine of our growth and profitability. It is, by almost any measure, the biggest, most profitable, highest-impact media business focused on preserving our environment, in the world. It's held that distinction almost continuously since its founding, by our predecessors John and Jane Shuttleworth, in 1970.

Today, about 6 million people regularly read *Mother Earth News*. And it's grown steadily, and profitably, the whole time we've had it.

That surprises some. In spite of its scale and longevity, *Mother*'s mixture of self-reliance and conservation-mindedness still strikes a lot of people as quaint. But I've never found it quaint. Since the first time I picked up a copy in the mid-1970s, I've thought *Mother*'s writing about small farms and energy-efficient technology forms a philosophical bedrock for humanity's relationship with its habitat.

Maybe that's because I learned my conservation from people like Tim Posey. Mr. Posey's personal values embraced all the definitions of "conservation." His home was a surplus building bought on the cheap from the US Army and moved to Anapra from Fort Bliss. Nearly every structure and every machine, every board and every wire on the Posey homestead was reclaimed, refurbished or repurposed. I'm sure that penchant for recycling was born of economic necessity. But part of what I learned from Tim Posey—and others like him—was that ingenious frugality could be the source of every bit as much intellectual satisfaction as any other form of invention. And a large part of that satisfaction, then as now, comes from the awareness that every power pole scavenged from a decommissioned railroad telegraph line saved a 30-year-old living tree from being cut down.

The fundamental values associated with conservation are virtually universal. Nearly every human being appreciates a living tree, and would like to save it from destruction.

And everyone likes a scavenger hunt. Hunting for a good, cheap used pole is more fun than going out and buying a new pole. When you offer people the chance to make constructive, creative changes in their own lives, most people are receptive.

Everyone wants to preserve clean air and water. Everyone likes a dose of nature now and then, in one form or another. Everyone wants future generations to be at least as prosperous, healthy and gratified as our generation. So why, I ask myself, has concern for the environment remained one of the most divisive topics on the American political agenda all my life?

In a word, fear.

My partners in arms—environmentalists—are afraid of the looming catastrophes. They have accepted their responsibility for humanity's impact on the planet. They know the data, and the data have a compelling story to tell. Earth's habitat is changing rapidly, and we are the cause. We are changing the atmospheric chemistry and the climate, depleting the groundwater, exhausting the topsoil and diminishing the planet's precious diversity of species.

Understandably, this knowledge fosters a sense of urgency. One doesn't have to contemplate our impact on the planet for very long before one starts to feel that we need to change our behavior in a major way—and soon. It's easy to feel a little freaked out.

On the other side of the geo-emotional divide are those who habitually deny that we are degrading the planetary environment. They've heard the murmuring about change, and instinctively recoil from the idea. If you plan to mention major societal change in any context, you can expect to get some recoil.

Both camps are fundamentally afraid of what tomorrow may bring. And both camps are motivated, to a destructive degree, by that fear.

Between these two camps sits a community of busy farmers, gardeners, goat-milkers, trail-builders, engineers, scientists, windmill climbers and solar installers. To a great degree they have led our society's journey toward sustainability, and they continue to do so.

They are leaders because their excitement is stronger than their fear.

Logically, when crisis threatens we need to subdue our fear in order to take constructive action. But taking action also somehow diminishes our fear. It feels natural. Once we get busy we're not as scared any more.

Perhaps we don't *control* the forces changing our climate when we grow a few vegetables, but we do *influence* those forces, and I think the activity profoundly changes our perspective. The situation immediately seems more manageable when we begin to manage.

That's been the most gratifying thing about my work, these past 30 years. My assignment, as I see it, is to get excited and stay excited about people who do good in the world—and the good they do. It's my job to tell their stories. In the process, I believe I've steadily become more optimistic. Probably as a side effect of the optimism, I even feel more energetic than I did 30 years ago, at least at work.

My work has been a sort of meditation on constructive action. And that meditation has made me feel more inclined to take constructive action myself.

I learned two important habits while I was a goat-milker and manure mixer on Tim Posey's homestead. First, Tim taught me how to connect with nature on a personal level. Animals are great models of constructive action. Their initiative is always authentic. They wake up every morning with a passion for living—until they die.

Tim Posey named nearly every animal on his place, even those he intended, eventually, to eat. He treated each of them with humane respect. He taught me how to handle the animals gently, and to let them show me how they wished to be treated. Chickens don't like sudden movements. Goats love to have their foreheads scratched, but a milk goat doesn't like cold hands or cold water on her udder, so we cleaned them off with warm water from the house. Tim showed me how you can swing a rabbit with its head down until it loses consciousness.

He always put them to sleep before he gave them one sharp blow with a hammer at the base of the skull. At his hands, I never saw one suffer.

Tim Posey taught me to respect the plants and animals we lived among and to understand their nutritional, medicinal and psychic values. He taught me to drink the goat's milk warm and to appreciate the companionship of the animals that provided it. Later I found other influences in the books of people like Wendell Berry, Robert Frost, Jane Goodall and Joel Salatin. Tim Posey led me there.

The second good habit I picked up on the Posey homestead was a natural inclination to get to work, and to do my work in a cheerful state of mind. There's an old cliché about busy hands being happy hands. It's a damned good cliché.

I'm sure passersby on Posey Road didn't generally share Tim's vision of paradise in the peeling paint and dry rot of his barns, but I learned to see the place through his eyes. Now I have my own place where the hinges are rusty and the garden overgrown, but I've preserved and developed a knack for seeing its charm and its grand potential. As I walk around the property, year after year, I can feel my tread getting a little slower, a little heavier, a little more in line with Tim's gait. And the habitual smile on my face is, maybe, a little more like Tim's smile.

I'm particularly grateful for the years I've spent with the tinkerers and visionaries who populate the pages of *Mother Earth News*. Tim Posey inducted me into his tribe of inventive, nature-loving crackpots. I feel very much at home in their company. Right now I'm editing a story about an Alabama farmer who powers his fleet of trucks with wood. He puts a charcoal burner on them and the motor burns the gases off the smoldering wood. No kidding. Another reader recently demonstrated how to heat a wall of your home with a homemade solar panel. In the same issue readers wrote in to explain how to make gazebos and birdbaths from old satellite dishes; how to turn cabinet doors into chalkboards; how to turn your old washing machine into a compost tumbler; and how your old flannel sheets can be turned into nice cloth diapers.

We're also writing about the dangers of genetically modified crops; gas wells that pollute groundwater; and plastic residues in canned food.

But most of the time we're doing our work with smiles on our faces.

Anne Tazewell

Anne Tazewell is fierce. And tireless. And although we occupy the same small "policy pond," which is renewable fuels in North Carolina, we haven't always worked well together.

When I entered the renewable fuels community Anne was busy winning big grant awards and paying money to petroleum companies to get them to incorporate renewables into their portfolios and infrastructure. I thought that was a lousy idea.

I thought we should put in place a 5 year "tax holiday" on biodiesel to make it more competitive at the pump. She thought a "holiday" was a ridiculous idea. And we fought about it hammer and tong.

But as the years passed a détente settled over us. I began to realize how complex the policy world is and how it is a difficult space to effect change. And in doing so I began to feel a begrudging respect for Anne. She's smart. And hardworking. And when her ideas fall off her shoulders and roll to the bottom of the mountain, she picks them up and starts heading for the summit all over again.

With time I started inviting Anne out to the plant. And with time I started stopping by Anne's office in Raleigh. When once I used to bash on the "renewables establishment," I am now part of it.

My respect for Anne spiked when working with her on using public monies. She is a crisp and efficient administrator—not something that can be said for everyone in the land of grants. Many grants are so poorly administered they are a good way for the awardee to go bankrupt.

Our meetings went from adversarial to commiserate, and we're both still in the game, years later, fighting to get renewable fuels into North Carolina's energy mix.

What was once a relationship focused solely on things like the Department of Transportation, or the Legislative Finance Committee, or our relationship with one politician or another, has evolved into stories of childhood, and talk of writing, and of the broader cause of which we are a part.

Here's Anne's take on the change she has wrought in the world. I think it is a fascinating tale...

SECRET AGENT
TO CHANGE AGENT

Anne E. Tazewell

It's fitting that I begin this exploration of my role as a change agent while riding the bus; my most recent effort to reduce my own carbon consumption. Even though I drive a Prius, the 70 miles round trip from home to my office consumes close to 1½ gallons of gasoline. After years of thinking it was too difficult to give up the freedom of driving to work, I've developed a great fondness for the time that bus travel allows for reading and ruminating. It's this extra time for contemplation that I credit, in part, to my growing awareness of the interconnectedness between my father's work as a secret agent and mine as a change agent.

My father walked away from our family when I was a child. I thought that his life as a spy had little to do with me. Now however I recognize the connections between his work to support the oil industry and my work to support the alternative fuels industry.

Since it took me so long to try the bus, I've grown to realize it's important to have patience with the many who don't give a thought to the 19 lbs of CO_2 emissions created by every gallon of gasoline burned, or make the connection to the blood spilled to keep our transportation system going. Now the bus time makes me feel relaxed and I have more patience with myself and the world around me.

If you are in the sustainability field for the long haul it's important to have patience. Humanity is evolving and there are forces greater than our individualistic, consumption-driven system that are conspiring to bring us to a higher consciousness; one in which we realize our divinity is in our unity. We are them; the ones that are raping the earth as well as the loving mother. I need to remind myself of this when I feel alienated and lonely.

Growing up I did not think much about my father. I saw him only a handful of times after he called it quits with my mother. Our first visit was shortly after she had moved my brother and me to Washington, D.C. following his announcement, via a letter written on a business trip to Europe that he was leaving her.

For all I know my father's death in 1989 went unannounced and unnoticed.

What I knew was that my parents had been married for nine years before I was born in Cairo and that my father worked for the CIA. I also knew that he consulted for the oil industry. In 1969 Miles Copeland, the man that had been my dad's partner, wrote a book titled *The Game of Nations*. A copy of the book sat on the basement book shelf of our D.C. home. Tucked inside the cover was an article from *Life* magazine, about their friend Kim Philby, the double agent who fled from Beirut to Moscow. While I may have glanced at the book over the years and even tried to read a bit here and there, it was never with any idea that these pages held any real importance to me.

Then, in 2002, my ears pricked up while listening to NPR on my way home from work. Some latent link was awakened between my father and me. Miles Copeland III was being interviewed about his new world music compilation. The interviewer asked about his earlier years and Miles mentioned his father's involvement in the CIA and how his brother's (Stewart) band The Police had been named because of their father's work in the Middle East. It dawned on me then to search for my father on the internet. Typing in James Eichelberger, CIA, I found a site hosted by ex "spooks" that led to Venn diagrams with varying colored lines drawn between different names to illustrate the intensity of their relationships. Red lines between people indicated a strong relationship, while blue illustrated a more distant connection. My father was close to Miles Copeland, Kim Roosevelt (the grandson of Teddy Roosevelt), Bill Eveland and many other players in the Middle East of the 1950s. Consequently I ordered *Ropes of Sand*, a biography by Eveland, because my father was mentioned in it.

Eveland described a trip that he and my father had taken to London in March 1956. MI6 was considering "taking out" then-president of Egypt, Gamal Abdel Nasser, claiming that he was a tool of the Russians. What I didn't realize was that, threatened by Nasser's populist rhetoric, Europe worried about their access to oil. A few short months later, Nasser denounced Western influence in the Arab world, and nationalized the Suez Canal. At the time, Britain had only three weeks of oil reserves, and the world began to choke on the intricate connections between Middle Eastern oil supplies and Western appetites.

I still hadn't fully made the connection between my work to reduce our dependence on imported oil and what my father had been doing to support it. More immediate things were on my mind than trying to make sense of the world my father had lived in—I still had two children at home, and we'd just moved away to North Carolina, where I'd accepted a new job as a Clean Cities coordinator.

Clean Cities is a US Department of Energy initiative begun in 1993 to bring together public and private partners to accelerate the use of alternative transportation fuels such as biodiesel, ethanol, electricity, propane and natural gas. The DOE conceived of this volunteer effort as a measure to promote energy security.

Previously I really hadn't given much thought to the fact that transportation accounted for ⅔ of our oil use and that close to 60% of US oil used was imported, much of it from countries hostile to us.

Not long after taking over, I experienced the bite of the Clean Cities Steering Committee. At one of our meetings the representative from Progress Energy brought me to tears by going on about how hybrid vehicles should not be considered alternative fuel vehicles; that they were not going to last and deserved no place in our efforts. On the other hand, I thought that by purchasing a Prius I was making an important statement about reducing our dependence on imported oil. Fortunately, the Duke Energy representative to the Steering Committee came to my rescue, agreeing after this incident to serve as the committee's chair. I was grateful for his kindness and frankly surprised at myself for shedding tears at a public meeting.

The tears were unprofessional for a "secret agent" gathering intelligence on a foreign element: career bureaucrats. I wanted to understand these people. In fact, I'd never had an office job before this, having worked as a restaurant owner, chef and textile artist before moving to North Carolina.

I opened a vegetarian restaurant in Norfolk, VA in 1976 where one of my early heroes was *Diet for a Small Planet* author, Francis Moore Lappe. Then, having moved to Key West in 1979 to have our first child, I rode the wave of the burgeoning recycling movement of the 1980s. A volunteer effort led by a group of young mothers was the beginning of our island community's first recycling center. We gathered tractor trailer loads of glass, plastic bottles, aluminum cans and paper which we had trucked to Miami.

I didn't go to college until after all three of my children had been born; after seven years I received an undergraduate degree in Environmental Studies. My commitment to creating a better world was born with my children, and I saw myself as someone outside of the mainstream. Now it had become increasingly important to me to try to work within the system to build bridges between different worlds to a more sustainable future. All of which brought me first to the Clean Cities committee, and later into state politics.

Given that one of the underlying tenets of my worldview is the belief that all likeminded souls are working together, I was surprised by my first foray into state politics. A bill sponsored in the North Carolina House to create a fund for the expansion of alternative transportation fuels received very little support from the environmental community. Even with the potential air quality benefits, there wasn't recognition from environmentalists that energy diversity in the transportation sector was a pillar of a more sustainable future. More troubling was the growing realization of how we've paralyzed our potential through endeavors that reflect Voltaire's astute observation that "the perfect is the enemy of the good."

None of the alternative fuel choices are without flaws but time spent quibbling among ourselves about which ones are worthy means that Big Oil can continue to keep us over a barrel. As someone now working on the "inside" as an advocate for the industry, the first time I saw the environmental groups' indifference toward alternative fuel, it hurt.

At the same time my commitment to compromise and communication was strengthened, especially towards those perceived as different from me: petroleum marketers, fleet managers and utility representatives.

After putting down my initial research on my father almost a decade ago to focus on family and career, I have now resumed my exploration with more earnestness, making personal acquaintances through the internet and reading several more pertinent books. Most recently, I've finally picked up Copeland's *The Game Player*. There's a chapter titled "Copeland and Eichelberger," where I learn that my father was behind their becoming consultants to Gulf Oil. They recognized a potential gold mine after learning in their first briefing with company executives that two thirds of Gulf's earnings came from oil in Kuwait, where Gulf was paying 10 cents a barrel and selling it at $1.85. My father and Miles parlayed their experience from earlier years as political operatives into becoming consultants by providing in-depth intelligence on the Kuwaiti royal family and the shifting sands of international relations. They used their time as CIA agents to build relationships across the Middle East, and they used Uncle Sam's money back at home, spreading greenbacks to keep in power those who were advantageous to the US and helping to get rid of those who were not. It was a game played to thwart Soviet influence in the region, but behind this was a focus on the increasing role that Middle Eastern oil would play in satisfying America's expanding appetites.

In a somewhat ironic twist, I also distribute money to influence change, but in the form of grants to public and private entities to help promote fuel diversity. Most of what I do is in the name of improved air quality as my primary source of funding is federal dollars reserved for counties that do not meet national air quality standards. In this role I have funded service station owners to add biofuel dispensers, truck stop owners to support truck stop electrification so big rigs can plug in rather than idle their engines overnight and fleet managers to use propane or compressed natural gas to reduce emissions and save up to 50% on fuel costs. What excites me most is working with people that hold different views than me. My soft spot is in supporting service station owners and fuel distributors. They are the "public face" of fuel choice and perhaps the most effective way to get off the path of Middle Eastern oil addiction—the path that my father helped pave.

On that path I have met and worked with some amazing people, many of whom are devising their own ways to further sustainability efforts.

Haddon Clark was my first introduction to a petroleum marketer interested in biofuels. Clean Cities had organized a meeting of alternative fuel advocates in the mountains, and Clark showed up with Earle Spruill, my ethanol mentor. All I remember now of the meeting was that he took us out to dinner in his new Cadillac equipped with heated leather seats. It's funny how memory can wrap itself in small wonders and creature comforts. United Energy, Haddon's company, went on to apply for funding from my program to support the first station in North Carolina to offer a B20 biodiesel blend in 2003. Regrettably Haddon didn't stick with selling the bio blend after the grant, which covered the cost between petro diesel and biodiesel, ran out. Nevertheless United Energy was a "bioneer," helping the Triangle region go from using 31,500 gallons of B20 in 2001 to at least 1.7 million gallons in 2004.

Lounell Mainor, from Magnolia, North Carolina, is a recent convert to biofuels. I first heard of her when a marketer I knew called to see if we knew of any E85 grant money for a new station in Duplin county—a place many in Raleigh would call "the other North Carolina;" an agricultural area struggling with a lack of opportunities for its young. Lounell wanted to do something for her community. I had never heard a petroleum marketer speak with such esteem about another business owner. Miz Lounell was born and raised on her family's farm where they grew corn, tobacco and soy. After attending college she spent a dozen years teaching and working as Assistant Register of Deeds, eventually getting into the funeral home business in the 1970s. Then, just a few years ago, she decided to launch a commercial service station in Duplin county.

That's when she contacted Dean Harrison of Abercrombie Oil who in turn contacted me. She had been working on this project for 6 years and wanted to add E85 to her new service station. When I recently asked Lounell why she wanted to add E85 she replied that this was a way to honor her parents' legacy as farmers, hopefully helping to provide an environment where crops such as corn could become more profitable for small farmers. Ethanol was cleaner and safer and she wanted to be the first to provide this fuel in her community.

Hill Oil is another marketer with a special place in my heart. They built Sparky's, a new E85 and B20 station 20 miles south of Winston-Salem. At the grand opening, Walter Hill and I were discussing the ups and downs of the biofuels business when he explained that the quickest, simplest way to fix our energy problem was to "pay the true price at the pump."

I finished the thought for him: Paying the true price would obviate the need for tax credits, grants, incentives and all the other inefficient boosts we give alternative fuels just so they can compete with hyper-subsidized petroleum fuels. It was so refreshing—I've never heard a petroleum marketer speak so frankly on the biggest barrier to the alternative fuels industry.

For me, the political challenge of ending oil dependency has become personal. By happenstance energy diversity has become the focus of my professional life while revealing a long-latent connection to my father. I want to counter my father's life shrouded in secrets by embracing my life in the light of possibilities.

I could have chosen to be embittered by my father's actions—instead, I'm inspired to use his same drive for change for a more equitable future. It's important not to underestimate the value of the grand scheme of things. We, as humans, are evolving. What once was considered fringe is becoming mainstream. By choosing open-source over closely held trade secrets; by opting for cooperation over competition; and by fostering energy diversity, we are creating more sustainable opportunities for growth.

Being an agent of change makes me hopeful. In some way, we all are continuing the story of our ancestors; it's in our DNA. The opportunity to evolve lies in how we choose to interpret and make use of inevitable change. I am honored to be able, in some small way, to help usher in a world of more transparency and considered consequences. They're not all perfect solutions but I am experiencing an evolution of consciousness and a breakdown of barriers. It's no longer us and them. We are one.

Glen Estill

Glen Estill is my older brother. He has me by about three and a half years, but he hasn't been able to beat me up for over thirty years. He's shorter. Grayer. And much smarter than me.

He's the reason I went into renewable energy. I can either thank him or blame him for my entry into the renewables establishment. His thought leadership has informed our thinking at Piedmont Biofuels, and today he is our second largest investor.

Glen and I have spent endless nights at one another's kitchen tables arguing, discussing and strategizing on ways to combat climate change. A breakthrough for one of us would lead to a breakthrough for the other. In some ways Lion's Head and Pittsboro are "sister cities." Both are small, both enjoy a mix of original residents and newcomers, and both have been characterized by our renewable energy projects.

While I was chronicling our journey into biodiesel in Energy Blog, Glen was silently putting up turbines. He later entered the blogosphere with his own Wind Blog.

When public sentiment toward wind energy in Ontario took a nasty turn, Wind Blog became an important battleground in the war of ideas, and it remains a platform which Glen uses to inform policy and public debate.

One big difference is that Glen sold his company and made a pot of money. At the time that he sold he had thirteen turbines spinning, making enough electricity to power about ten thousand Canadian homes. Along the way he contributed to the shaping of Ontario's wind industry.

Nowadays he is a "retired guy," who spends a fair bit of each winter living in a small solar powered "bunkey" in our side yard in North Carolina. It's a shame that he refuses to write the story of how he made a lot of money in renewable energy. I often argue that "getting his story out there" would be an excellent way to demonstrate how it is possible to do well while doing good.

Unlike me Glen does not reach for the limelight. Some might regard him as shy. I've watched him weather the anti-wind lobby as it has summoned its forces, complete with vitriol, nuclear power plant workers, and misinformation campaigns.

Since his successful exit from the wind business, Glen has been quietly serving on boards, informing policy makers, and contributing behind the scenes to the renewable electricity conversation which is currently swirling about Ontario.

He continues to assist us with both our operations and our thinking at Piedmont Biofuels, and I think his story is an important one to consider when thinking about how to effect societal change...

SKY GENERATION

Glen Estill

You remember the time of your first born. For me, it was November 27, 2002 at 10:36 PM. I was home watching the news when the phone rang. "We are producing power," said Jason, project manager for Vestas, the supplier of the wind turbine. A wave of happiness combined with relief passed over me. A project, more than two years in the making, was coming to completion.

Weeks earlier, I had been told the turbine would be operating by November 15. I wanted to host a party to acknowledge the help I had received from so many people. I selected November 30—hopefully soon enough to avoid winter weather, but enough time to ensure an operating turbine.

Annette designed the invitations. They were printed and sent. The Lioness Club was hired to do the food. Rotary Hall was booked, and the Rotary Club was engaged to run the cash bar. The Bruce Peninsula Environment group wanted to help, and so Don and Bob helped park cars. Mayor Milt McIver and Council were invited. Ovid Jackson, Member of Parliament, Bill Murdoch, Member of Provincial

Parliament, and Steve Gilchrist, the Commissioner of Renewable Energy were invited.

Paul Duff, a local artist, was commissioned to do a painting—a wind turbine under a rainbow—as a gift for the municipal office. My brother Lyle was commissioned to make some metal sculptures of kites for gifts. A kite flying club from Guelph was invited, and accommodations arranged for them.

A press release had been sent to the local paper announcing the event. The whole community was invited. The details had been looked after. I asked Tom Boyle, a local councilor, if he thought anybody would come. He thought they would.

We missed the impending winter deadline by a day. The day of the grand opening, November 30, saw a bitterly cold first winter storm from the northwest. The wind howled, and snow pelted across the field at the wind turbine where we did tours. Several visitors on the way from the south turned around because of bad winter driving conditions, missing the event. But people came. A lot of people. Cars were lined up all the way down the kilometer-long driveway. The police stopped to direct traffic at the highway. The lineups for tours at the turbine were so long that Jim Salmon, a long time consultant to the wind business volunteered on the spot to help. Two local kids, Ryan and Carter, cut the ribbon. I had to help them hold the ribbon, the wind was so strong. Photos were hurriedly taken. Then we headed to Rotary Hall for speeches, presentations and camaraderie.

The hall was packed. My younger brother Lyle and his family, and my older brother Mark from North Carolina. Mom and Dad. Old friends from my Guelph and Woodstock days, and new friends on the Peninsula. Suppliers, shareholders and contractors. Emerson McLay, the landowner who leased his land for the turbine, and his family. Emerson's neighbors. Bruce Peninsula Environment Group members. Renewable energy supporters. As only the 9th commercial-scale wind turbine in the Province of Ontario, and only the second one built by the private sector, this was a big deal.

I was introduced by a long time friend, Tim Matheson, who lives near the turbine, and who originally introduced me to Emerson, and offered a place to stay when I visited the site. "I've known Glen since we were 10 years old at Camp Bimini," he said. "There aren't many people who have the integrity, the drive, and the determination to build something like this. Glen knows we need to reduce our use of fossil fuels, and instead of just whining about it, he is doing something about it. Glen is someone who puts his money where his mouth is."

I introduced Mayor McIver, who said, "I first spoke to Glen about this project back in early 2001. And now here we are. This project came in without any opposition at all. We welcome this."

Steve Gilchrist spoke. "Glen has built the biggest erection on the Bruce Peninsula." My Peninsula friends got a kick out of that one, and have introduced me that way ever since (though they usually leave out a word). The local members of Parliament spoke and presented a framed certificate congratulating my firm on the milestone. Then I spoke for a few minutes. "Ontario currently gets 25% of its power from burning coal. When the wind is blowing, Ontario won't need to burn as much coal to supply the Peninsula with power.

This one turbine will supply enough to power 500 homes on average. There will be less climate change, less smog, and less acid rain. It is only a start, but it is an important start."

I thanked my shareholders. I thanked Vestas, Tiltran, Boyle Concrete, Bernie Hellyer Construction and other contractors. I saved the best for last.

"There is one person I want to thank especially. Two years ago, I approached him to put up a meteorological tower on his land to measure winds. Anyone else might have just asked if this guy was crazy—there just weren't any turbines operating in the Province. I can't say enough about how good he and his family have been to deal with. Please welcome Emerson McLay to the stage."

The crowd went nuts, and flash bulbs flashed. You have to understand that Emerson was never one to seek attention. And he was not one for public speaking. But he graciously thanked the ladies in the kitchen, and me. And I know he was proud of his project.

Tami, my sister-in-law, was standing in the balcony beside my Mom. "How proud are you of Glen now?" My mother came close to crying. The warmth in that room on a frigid afternoon was overwhelming. Renewable energy was coming to Ontario. There was a feeling that we weren't hopeless in the fight against climate change. There were possibilities for cleaning up the air. It could happen. Solutions existed, and we just need to get on with deploying them.

My journey into wind had begun in the summer of 1999. I had a more than full-time job in Guelph working for our family's wholesale computer company. I had been working there for 20 years, and was getting a bit burned out. So I took a sabbatical for a summer. One of my activities during my time off was a camping trip to Newfoundland.

I have vivid memories of the wind in Newfoundland. We would put a tarp up over the picnic table at the campsite, and find it 3 campsites away when we returned from a walk. It was windy all the time. I kept thinking there must be something you could do with the energy in the wind. I had read a piece on wind energy in a newsletter from the Suzuki Foundation, and now what had been an abstract thought was blowing across my face.

When I returned home, I began researching wind on the Internet. It turned out Denmark had a flourishing wind business, and was getting a significant share of their power from wind. Canada's first wind farms had gone up in Pincher Creek, Alberta, and later in Gaspe, Quebec. I knew that Ontario was in the process of deregulating the power business, moving from the single government owned supplier, Ontario Hydro, to what would supposedly be a market based system. Perhaps what the wind business needed in Ontario was a business person to apply their skills to it. I left the family business in May of 2000 to chase the wind.

By November of 2000, I had established a handshake arrangement with Emerson McLay, my landowner. Jim Salmon's firm, Zephyr North, erected a meteorological tower on Emerson's property to measure the winds. Once you measure the winds, you can estimate production, and from there, come up with a financial model for a business plan.

But there was just one problem. The business plan didn't work. The price of power was too low to justify investment. It did not earn enough to pay a fair return to investors. The project would not get the needed capital.

I consider stubbornness a virtue, and nowhere is this a more necessary virtue than in the wind business. I began doing more research. I read the wind trade press, books on wind, and attended conferences, to learn all I could. I spoke to others in the business, and even took a trip to Denmark to talk to manufacturers and turbine owners.

At one of the conferences I learned about marketing green power. A certain percentage of people will pay a premium price for electricity from green sources. It made sense to me. After all, I was quitting a good paying job, where all of my business experience came from, to take a leap into an unknown business. And I was doing it because I thought it needed to be done. Surely some people would agree, and would pay a premium for their power.

I started discussions with several retailers of electricity. In 1999, the government had deregulated the electricity market. The price of electricity was supposed to change with market forces—supply and demand. Of course the market structure had big problems. The government-owned Ontario Power Generation (OPG) had over 70% market share, and the second largest supplier, Bruce Power, was renting a multi-billion dollar nuclear plant from OPG for almost nothing, while leaving OPG with the responsibility of dealing with the waste. It wasn't exactly a free market. But retailers were allowed, and they were soliciting contracts from consumers. Their big pitch was a three- or five-year fixed price contract. Consumers who didn't want the risk of price changes in the "free" market could lock in. Telemarketers and door-to-door sales forces sprang into action.

Surely some of these retailers would like to launch a green power product. I spoke to a number of them, and they were all interested. But they didn't know how much they could sell. And they didn't think they could sell until they had supply. It was a chicken and egg problem. I prepared a business plan based on the likelihood of selling power at a premium through retailers. And I took it to a number of friends and associates, to see if they would be interested in investing.

Raising the capital was the easy part for me. I was investing a substantial portion of my net worth, and I structured the company so that my pay was only 2% of revenues. My income would be very low unless the company grew. I think it was this personal commitment by me that made it easy for investors to get on board.

My first turbine was built using the Canadian Renewable Conservation Expense, which allowed the investment to be deducted from the investor's income. This motivated investors with high tax rates. Of course it sounds better than it was—it made the cost zero for tax purposes, so a larger capital gains liability existed if we sold the company. Some of the investors thought it was the right thing to do to invest in a green initiative. They wanted results that weren't just financial. I always brag that I spent about $300 on lunches to raise the needed $3.6 million. It was a private offering, and I had 17 participants.

The turbine supply agreement was not so easy. I was a very little company with no track record in the business. I had difficulty getting calls returned. Vestas was the only firm in the province that had local service—I knew that was the way I had to go. I travelled to the Canadian Wind Energy Association conference in Vancouver, which was a small event attended by 300 people. At their booth, I ambushed the Vestas sales manager for Canada. After a few minutes of discussion, he realized that I might be able to pull it off. Wind turbine vendors at the time had a lot of "do good" tire kickers, who wanted to build a wind turbine, but who had no idea how to go about it. No wonder vendors didn't return calls. We formed a solid relationship.

The agreement was a long document. It filled a 3 inch 3 ring binder, and covered just about every eventuality. I was responsible for the road, and the electrical infrastructure. Vestas would build the foundation, tower and turbine. The agreement included a service contract.

The biggest challenge was dealing with the local utility, provincially owned Hydro One. Of course, I was new at this, and so were they. They seemed to make up rules on the fly, then they'd change them. Then they'd describe the rule as a "standard." I wondered how that could be when the rules were changing all the time. Since when is a standard based on a whim? Add all that to a boilerplate "take it or leave it" connection agreement, which covered them, but left the customer exposed. Supposedly they were protecting the integrity of their system. But there's no discussion, no arguing with them. Even if you did argue, it didn't matter. It was "standard."

Obtaining permits to build the turbine was challenging. I had to prepare an environmental assessment. This involved consulting with neighbors, the municipality and First Nations, various Federal and Provincial Ministries, and preparing a report on the local environment, including social, economic, endangered species, water, soil, land use, etc. The report was reviewed by Natural Resources Canada (NRCan). I prepared some verbiage on the impact of the turbine on climate change. When the turbine was producing, the province could burn less coal to make electricity, saving 4,500,000 kgs of CO_2 emissions. NRCan asked me to revise my report, and include this only as an appendix. Apparently a project is to be assessed only on its own impacts, and the impact on the electricity system as a whole is considered unimportant. Or maybe it is climate change that is unimportant.

Permits were obtained from Nav Canada and Transport Canada for aeronautic lighting. From the Ministry of Transportation for the road entrance. From the municipality for the building permit.

Today, the permitting is far more difficult. I prepared the environmental assessment report myself, with about 3 weeks of research. Today, I would need consultants to prepare the report. The rules are always changing, and the list of those who need to be consulted is much more prescriptive, and extensive. I have become deeply skeptical of the environmental assessment process. It adds cost, and time, and very little value. I am not aware of the environmental assessment process ever making a significant change to anything. Somehow, people are allowed to build new transmission, refurbish nuclear plants with their known waste storage problem, and build new coal or natural gas plants, with their vast carbon emissions. They're able to build tar sand extraction operations that scar the earth, pollute the water, and have enormous carbon, sulfur and nitrogen oxide emissions. How exactly does the environmental assessment protect the environment? All these other power projects required the same process, and they, too, were allowed in the end.

Finally, after all the permits were in place, the business plan prepared, the capital raised, the turbine supply agreement signed, and the construction completed, the turbine was operating.

But the business plan was in shambles. The Provincial government, facing an election, was getting political pressure due to rising electricity prices. On November 11, 2002, the government froze electricity prices. The next day, electricity retailers—my prospective customers—all closed their doors. After all, why would a consumer buy a 3 year fixed-price contract when the government already guaranteed a fixed price? Selling the electricity at a premium was going to be a challenge. I learned my first hard lesson in the electricity business. All that matters is government policy.

The celebration for the suppliers, shareholders, neighbours and community was well-deserved. But I secretly had concerns about the project's viability.

It took almost 3 years before I was able to obtain the premium price on the electricity I was producing, but I finally got there. Bullfrog Power finally opened up, and the company was able to expand with contracts in place to sell the premium power.

By 2009 wind energy had enemies. One advertisement in a local newspaper had a headline which read: "Wind Turbine Syndrome. What they (Wind Turbine Tycoons) don't tell us about wind turbines." It went on to read, "Are wind turbines a clean source of energy? NO, they are not. It is a known fact for 10 years or more that wind turbines are a health hazard.... The Bruce nuclear plant still runs at 100% capacity..."

I was stunned. Where had this come from? Were these known facts? "Wind turbine tycoon" didn't really fit with my self-image. I wondered, "Will people believe this nonsense?" Surely no one would believe "Bruce nuclear plant at 100% capacity" since two of its eight units had been off-line since the 1990s. How can they just make this stuff up?

Then I received a flyer distributed at a meeting in my community of Lion's Head. "Those who deliberately mislead others about the virtues of wind power are not your friends. They are simply profiteers seeking to advance their owner self-interests."

Profiteer? I left a high paying job, where I could easily have made more money. I sacrificed to build the wind business. I thought, "Mislead about wind power? Me? No, they have that backwards."

I was taken aback by the vicious, factually incorrect, and personal attacks by these opponents of wind. Tactics like this divide communities and spread fear; they are classic propaganda techniques. I thought of Joseph Goebbels who once said "If you tell a lie big enough and keep repeating it, people will eventually come to believe it."

The anti-wind forces are well-funded. They challenge the professional credentials of anyone who speaks in favor of wind, in order to silence them. They use strategic lawsuits against public participation, to intimidate and stifle those who want sustainable wind energy.

I understand it better now. The root of misinformation disseminated by the opponents of wind comes from reports from right-wing think tanks or participants supported by the fossil and nuclear industry. This misinformation causes genuine concerns among some people.

Wind is the fastest-growing source of new electricity generation capacity in Europe, and second-fastest after natural gas in the US. There was no new coal capacity added in Europe in 2010, and almost none in the US. Nuclear is going backwards fast since Fukushima. If the current trends continue, wind will be the dominant source of power in the world in 30–40 years. The status quo is threatened. And historically, has there ever been a better way to defend that status quo than to blunt the competition?

From the Environmental Defense Canada website, October 4, 2011: "A union well-known for its aversion to green energy has been caught faking a grassroots campaign, attacking renewable energy while promoting the nuclear and coal industries in Ontario. As was revealed yesterday in a damning report from PostMedia News. The Ontario Power Workers' Union paid a major PR firm to create numerous blogs and anonymous social media accounts questioning the viability of renewable energy, while promoting a 'diverse mix of energy sources,' including nuclear and coal."

I find it unbelievable. A simple business idea—to harness the wind to make electricity—has engendered a brutal societal debate. As an early adopter in Ontario, I have no choice but to enter the fray—which means my language and approach has to shift to a battle footing.

Make no mistake. We are in a war with entrenched vested interests to shift the world to a sustainable energy path. And the first casualty of war is the truth. We have no choice but to win this war, and so we will. With truth. With technology and cost improvements. With science. We must not sit on our hands and let the world drift towards environmental destruction. It is up to me. It is up to you.

For me the change in perception from being loved and respected by all, to a vilified profiteer damaging the earth has been painful. When you truly believe in something, you just can't understand how others don't agree with you. And it is always easier to be loved than hated.

Making change is not easy, and not without controversy. But change we must.

Nicola Ross

I barely know Nicola Ross. But just as my brother Glen took a break from his technology job and found himself in the wind business, Nicola is a big proponent of sabbaticals.

I first met her at the Bookshelf Café in Guelph, Ontario. At the time she was publishing a journal called *Alternatives: Environmental Ideas + Action*. I was doing a reading at the Bookshelf, to support my second book, *Small Is Possible; Life in a Local Economy*, and the organizers of the event arranged for Nicola to introduce me.

As I watched Nicola on stage, her passion for environmental issues was evident. The crowd knew her. Her peer-reviewed journal was the gold standard for Canadian environmental activism. I was intrigued.

A year later I submitted an article to *Alternatives* on grassroots biodiesel production. The article was accepted, subject to peer review, and I snickered. I wondered who on earth they could find who would know more about grass-roots biodiesel than me. But when the reviews came in I was shocked. The criticisms were sharp, and accurate. My biases were exposed along with my false claims. I was stunned. The process of publishing with her improved my writing, and my thinking a lot.

Nicola has used her words as her foremost weapon in her desire for change. She's an award winning author with four books and many newspaper and magazine articles to her credit, and I think her story can be an important corner-stone when thinking about effecting change...

ON SABBATICAL

Nicola Ross

Suddenly I'm aware of my clammy underarms. Droplets of sweat slither down my back gaining momentum until they catch on the waistband of my khaki trousers. But the perspiration gives me no relief from the blast of tropical heat that marks the end of Managua's Sandino Airport's air-conditioned sanctuary and the beginning of my Nicaraguan adventure.

Other passengers' family members and friends push anxiously against the floor-to-ceiling tinted-glass walls that separate them from their loved ones. I find myself looking for a familiar face in the pressing crowd, a stranger, even, holding up a handwritten sign that bears my name. Knowing that there is no one here to welcome me makes me feel very much alone.

Beyond these Nicaraguans' uniformly black hair, dark eyes and unblemished toffee-colored skin, beat-up taxis, minibuses and immense Toyota Land Cruisers rush by only to slow for the next speed bump. They honk for no apparent reason, belching clouds of particulate-laden exhaust as they accelerate toward some imaginary finish line. The fumes obscure the bougainvillea-draped wall that is the backdrop to this mayhem. The enormous clusters of flowers are vibrant orange and purple, but mostly fuchsia.

I'm not yet ready to step into the unknown world beyond those glass doors. So I swing my knapsack back to the floor to make some unnecessary adjustments. Anything to buy me a bit more time within the airport's cool anonymity and out of reach of my future.

Never before when I traveled have I experienced the near panic that seems to be sucking those cold droplets of sweat back up between my shoulder blades, and making me wince at my decision to come on this excursion. But then, never before have I ventured out on my own to a developing country—or any country for that matter—on a self-awarded sabbatical. If I didn't recognize before that traveling alone in an unknown land might be hard, it strikes me now.

I step through the smoky glass door into my new, if impermanent, life.

I wrote those words in early 2004 as I began my second self-awarded sabbatical. In re-reading them, I wonder: What possessed me to want to venture alone to that war-torn Central American country? What drove me to it? Why would I abandon the Caledon Countryside Alliance, the small, nonprofit organization I'd created six years earlier and had built into an effective voice that was helping protect my local community from development pressures? Why had I decided to push my boundaries so far and in this way? And had it been worth it?

The impetus to set out on my own, I knew, grew from the stunning experience I'd had with my first year off, about seven years earlier.

The hollowed out cargo van, long past its prime, drops us off at the edge of a harvested cornfield on a steep slope. As our transport had climbed up the twisting, rocky road to this spot, afternoon clouds had given way to thickening fog. Despite the cold dampness, the air is fresh as we scramble out of the van. It revives our travel-weary bones. We've been on the go for close to 12 hours, all of it in some form of Mexico's second-class transportation system.

With night coming along quickly, as it does in southerly climes, we have only a vague idea of where we are and, more importantly, where we are going. The driver waves vaguely indicating that the familia Pedraza lives somewhere below the field of harvested maize. "Follow the path," he adds.

After hoisting our backpacks, we discover what appears to be a trail through the furrows, and begin our descent in the deep soil and thick mist. The grim evening is as comforting as a Jack the Ripper movie shot in a London fog. With our heads down, intent on not tripping over clods of earth, we are slow to pick up on the melodic singing that begins to penetrate the gloom. Instinctively, we follow the music until we make out the alto voice of Loreena McKennitt singing her Celtic tunes. We fail to note the irony that we are hiking in Mexico's Sierra Gorda Mountains listening to the sounds of a Canadian singer/songwriter waft through the row of towering gum trees that line the cornfield. But as if it were a scattering of breadcrumbs, we track the melody to the home of Paty Ruiz Corzo, her husband Roberto Pedraza and their two sons, Beto and Mario. We are certain that no one but this inspiring Mexican family would be playing this music in this place at this time.

Enveloped in darkness, we pass through a vaguely familiar wooden gate (We had been here once before though we'd arrived from below rather than above.) and we can make out a low-slung wooden house. Inside, flickering candles and a dim light powered by a few solar panels provide the first feeling of warmth we've had in some time. Murmuring voices intermingle with the soft thud-thud of someone chopping vegetables. Seconds later, we are hugging our friends. They are the heart and soul of Grupo Ecologico Sierra Gorda, the non-governmental organization that will eventually inspire me to create the Caledon Countryside Alliance.

It may come as no surprise that a Mexican NGO would be the model I used to create a non-profit organization in Canada, but that my first year-long sabbatical would have this outcome certainly ran adrift from what I'd expected from those 12 months of freedom from the shackles of a working life. When I was in my mid-thirties, an international contract inspired me to take a year's leave from Calgary, where I'd been living and working for 16 years. The 18-month gig had involved extensive travel to Latin America, where I'd managed a major project that transferred environmental know-how between Canada and 22 national petroleum companies in 18 Latin American and Caribbean countries. It gave me an appetite for international work and was a world apart from running an NGO in the Southern Ontario town where I grew up.

I decided that when the contract ended, in March 1994, I would invest a year to go live "in-country," as the international lingo goes, improve my Spanish and be ready to advance my environmental career by working with organizations such as the Canadian International Development Agency, the World Bank, United Nations Development Programme and more. First, however, I would have to divest myself of EnviroLine, the subscription-based environmental newsletter I'd created in 1989 that had taken root in Western Canada's energy and forestry sectors. Fortunately, my managing editor was up to the task. She purchased the small business, leaving me free to escape.

About a year later, in August, my partner Neil and I climbed aboard an airplane. In my back pocket, I had a small contract to do some climate change investigative work in Peru, but first, Neil and I would walk across the Rio Grande from Texas into Mexico and make the long trip to the home of the Incas by train, bus and airplane. We had brand new packs on our backs, some money in the bank and no schedule except a loose agreement to be high in the Andes come November.

Though my day planner had no entries, I had an agenda of another sort. This year would be my ticket to the next phase of my environmental career. It would be fun, but more importantly, it would be a steppingstone up—my version of an MBA.

The year lived up to its billing. It was fun. My personal history book will record 1995/96 as one of the best periods of my life. It was also life-changing. I successfully completed my contract in Peru, and though we'd planned to stay on in this South American nation, Neil and I caught a flight back to Mexico, a country that we'd come to love in the short few months we'd travelled there. That we chose Mexico over Peru would be the first of a number of decisions that I never would have predicted in advance. But this colorful, lively place had spoken to our hearts, and we listened to them— something that seldom happens when you are ensconced in a Canadian career.

During our time in Mexico, I worked at a small weekly English-language newspaper, and Neil taught English. More importantly, we came to know Grupo Ecologico Sierra Gorda. While we helped them set up a forestry project intended to battle climate change, I watched what this group did, how they did it and the passion they had for the Sierra Gorda, a mountainous region that is now a UNESCO Biosphere Reserve. Their commitment to and belief in the need to protect their home infected me; it inspired me.

Nonetheless, I returned to Canada still intent on developing an international consulting practice. I thought I'd hit the jackpot when I was selected to be the climate change expert on a three-person team hired to evaluate the first phase of the Global Environment Facility. The contract took me to Washington, DC; New York City; Zimbabwe; and the Philippines. I thought: This is it. I've made it. My yearlong investment has paid off.

So no one was more surprised than me with my pronouncement when I completed that contract. I vowed that it would be a long time before I'd be back on a plane visiting international projects. What I'd seen in Washington, New York and abroad so disturbed me that I wanted no part of the corruption. What I really wanted to do was to start my own version of Grupo Ecologico Sierra Gorda in Caledon, the Ontario town where I'd grown up. A year later, I was living back home and had incorporated the Caledon Countryside Alliance (CCA) as a non-governmental organization with a mandate to protect this lovely area that is situated within Toronto's urban shadow. The CCA would give the land a voice, helping to protect it from the housing developments that threatened its rolling hills, its rocky landscape, the Niagara Escarpment, the Oak Ridges Moraine, its lakes and rivers and small villages.

More than once in the ensuing years, I would shake my head at the unexpected outcome of my year's leave. From international consultant to running a small NGO in my hometown. From Calgary to Caledon, a 2,000-mile journey. From worrying about other places and other cultures to recognizing how much there was to be done in my own backyard. I vowed that every seven years I would repeat the sabbatical, force my eyes open, challenge myself and, in this way, seek inspiration.

As the years ticked by, I was totally caught up in my work with the Caledon Countryside Alliance and with my budding writing career. I'd had some success in publishing environmental articles and was coming to understand the power of the pen in Caledon's environmental battles. I was too busy and too engaged to consider leaving this life, though from time to time I did ponder what had caused me to go to Mexico and Peru. Hard as I'd try, though, I couldn't understand what had possessed me to do something so rash.

Then one day, the fire was back in my belly. I have no idea why it returned or exactly when, but I found myself reading travel literature, drooling over other people's distant adventures. I convinced myself that I'd accomplished enough of what I'd hoped to do with the Caledon Countryside Alliance, and that its future growth and maturation would be best left in the hands of others.

I was off, and this time, I was off on my own. Off to Nicaragua, home of the Sandinistas, Daniel Ortega, and some of the loveliest Spanish colonial cities on the small subcontinent. It was a war-torn, dirt-poor nation with little

infrastructure for tourists. Though I tried to avoid predict-
ing the outcome of my stay, I hoped to do something other
than save the environment. After about 20 years working in
the sector, it was time for a break.

One cold January day, Neil drove me to the airport and
I boarded a plane headed for Managua. A few hours later,
I was alone in the Sandino Airport with that sweat pour-
ing down my back, looking out at hoards of waiting Nicaraguans. What was I doing, I wondered? What inspiration was
to be found in this foolish undertaking?

Then I came across a book by Sara Wheeler called *Travels in a Thin Country: A Journey Through Chile*, in which the
author travels the length of that skinny country. She com-
bines her tales of some gutsy travel with information about
the country's natural and cultural history. I could do that I
decided. I could do the same thing here in Nicaragua. I could
touch the four corners of this box-shaped country, and so I
did. I travelled by bus, ox-cart and on foot. I lived in First
Nation communities, visited Nicaragua's version of the "wild
west." I travelled in the footprints of the Sandinistas, saw the
bullet-ridden buildings, spoke with Nicaraguans who had
been traumatized by the 1972 earthquake that obliterated
downtown Managua with an intensity that rivaled Haiti's in
2010. I travelled down rivers by dugout canoe and endured
proselytizing preachers on overcrowded buses. In the end,
I saw every damn corner of that fascinating and welcoming
country. It was terrifying and exhilarating. More than once,
beads of sweat travelled the length of my back, but I touched
the four corners convinced that I'd find a publisher for this
book, my fourth.

In the last days of my time in Nicaragua, I was in an Internet cafe checking messages. One stood out. Would I be interested in the job of editor of *Alternatives Journal*, wrote Bob Gibson, an environmental professor at the University of Waterloo and the environmental magazine's longtime editor? I didn't know Bob well, so the offer came out of the blue.

Rather than accept the job though, I spent the next two years trying to shed my environmental career. I wanted to do something less ridden with doom-and-gloom. Maybe I could become a travel writer. I returned to Nicaragua to research an article about a dark spooky ailment called Grisi Siknis that primarily afflicts young Miskito women. I celebrated the day it appeared in *The Walrus* magazine, a publication that only takes the best of the best. I honed my writing and editing skills. I taught journalism at a community college. But hard as I worked on the manuscript for my Nicaraguan book, it was never published.

What I did discover, however, is that sustainability, climate change, biodiversity and other environmental concerns had become part of my DNA. When the editor's role at *Alternatives* came up again, I didn't just give in to the double helix that carries my genetic code, I jumped in with both feet. I would combine my journalism skills with my environmental passion.

Much of the job involves working with really smart people on fascinating environmental topics. What could be more engaging? My learning curve climbed into the stratosphere as I did my best to turn complex environmental ideas into interesting and digestible prose. The magazine improved both editorially and stylistically. *Alternatives* is the only Canadian publication dedicated to dealing intelligently and creatively with environmental ideas that matter. Not a source of news, it is an analytical journal that is enjoyable to read and wonderful to look at.

I thought my love affair with the magazine would go on forever, and for a long time it did. But as 2011 approached, seven years after my Nicaraguan adventure, my mind began to stray from *Alternatives'* pages. My daydreams would be of far-off places and different tasks rather than the article I happened to be editing. My version of the seven-year itch had returned.

As I write this, I sit at a table overlooking the small coastal village of Cuastecomate. I'm back in Mexico, home of my first inspiring year's sabbatical. It's late December and I'm less than a month into my new adventure. I'm not alone this time. In less than two weeks, we will be off to Argentina. I'll spend the summer months back in Canada on the historic French River helping organize an outfitting business. Canoes and kayaks will replace much of my time spent with pen and paper. My writing these days has shifted from the environment to sport, another of my passions. I can see myself becoming a travel-sport writer—surely some magazine will be interested in a story about playing polo or fly fishing in Argentina. I await publication of an article I wrote for *Explore* magazine about my two-week adventure last summer paddling the Northwest Territories' challenging Mountain River.

I know better than to predict where I might be and what I might be doing a year from now, after twelve months spent mostly free from the day-to-day rigors of a nine-to-nine job. I know that inspiration arrives in unexpected ways and, if you let it, will take you on unanticipated journeys. I also suspect that while my mind has turned to sport, my passion about the environment has not abated. It will likely resurface, though I dare not predict the form it will take.

Awarding oneself a sabbatical every seven years isn't for everyone. There are lots of other ways to find inspiration. But of one thing I'm sure: inspiration comes through challenge. It happens when you get out of your comfort zone, when you plunk yourself down in territory so uncertain that it causes cold sweat to rise up between your shoulder blades and slither slowly down your back.

Gary Phillips

Gary Phillips is a big southern bear of a man. He likes to hug people. And he hugs hard. As a middle aged Canadian with failing eyesight, I tend to carry my eyeglasses around by a strap that lets them hang onto my chest. I have to be careful when I greet Gary. He tends to hug so hard my eyeglasses break.

Gary is eclectic. As a politician he's gone from adored to vilified, and back again. As an auctioneer he is masterful. As a preacher he marries folks and buries folks with equal solemnity and grace.

I first read one of Gary's essays in *Radio Free Bubba*, and I have long been a fan of his poetry ever since.

I have a hard time putting Gary in the proper cubby hole. One moment he is tearing up over a ritualistic summoning of the four directions, and the next he is downing moonshine with abandon. He's part sensitive new age guy, part hillbilly, part Morehead scholar, and part activist. He's rather impossible to pin down.

One day I bumped into Gary at the General Store Café in Pittsboro. He was alone, downing a glass of champagne, reading a book, with a pile of books on his table. I pulled up a chair. I was alone, downing a beer, with a backlog of emails to contend with.

He was celebrating. A deal he had been working on had broken its log jam and to honor the occasion he had gone to the Friends of the Library Book Sale, bought a bunch of titles, and settled into some champagne.

Gary and I have a strange and twisted relationship. When he was in politics I was a supporter. We threw parties for him and contributed to his campaigns. As a preacher he helped us bury my brother Mark, for which our family is forever grateful. And as a preacher he is the only person who has ever welcomed me into communion, at an ecumenical church service he performs twice a year at the Shakori Festival of Music and Dance.

I've never been confirmed in a church. Which has kept the holy sacraments off limits. Gary has a different take on that. He's happy to turn the church teachings upside down to welcome someone in.

Gary joined me on a "grease run," where we vacuumed out the used cooking oils of various restaurants. The day we did that he ordered a glass of Proseco with lunch.

I never know what my relationship to Gary is. Sometimes I'm his pupil. Sometimes I'm his peer. When I am on stage at the poetry slam with him we are competitors. And when we are sharing a flask of whiskey at the Coffee Barn we are simply friends.

Gary has forgotten more about societal change than I will ever know, and here is his story…

ALL ROUND ACTIVIST

Gary Phillips

We can do no great things, only small things with great love.
« MOTHER TERESA »

I was born into a great sprawling multi-racial family that ran from the mountains of North Carolina down to the Cherokee foothills of South Carolina. We identified ourselves mostly as poor, Southern and white, but I knew from the time I was 5 or 6 years old that the color line was more like my mother's clothes line, with a wide range of shades flapping in that breeze.

We were hill-and-mountain people who lived in the open—hunters; farmers; preservers of food, old stories and fierce family love. The legacy for me was a world where nature was never outside somewhere but connected with strong cords to my heart and my breath and to the soles of my feet, to the common daily adventures of a wondrous world.

At major family gatherings I usually had a choice; I could go out hunting or tinkering with the men or I could stay with the women and the cooking and their stories. Often I held with the women, and that shaped my life.

I am in a camp somewhere between Wendell Berry and Derek Jensen, home-centered and nourishing but near to rage at the stupidity and culpability of the world's extractive economy, its overarching patriarchy and grinding impulse to empire.

These days I think of myself as a kind of spiritual janitor. I write; I live in an elegant dirt-house built by people I love; I walk the woods. I facilitate the transitions of organizations, negotiate the transfer of land, carry water for strong women, create rituals and perform liturgies. I bind people together and honor their dead. I pray for the soil under my feet and call in the directions in ceremony. I listen to trees and every living thing. Sometimes I give a public and powerful witness; sometimes it scares people. I give good solid advice. I love my partner. I cook, and I clean up.

My sweet mother is Mary June Holloway and she still lives in the house I grew up in, the last survivor of a dozen rough-scrabble brothers and sisters. Hers was a high-mountain clan colored with Cherokee. They owned 46 acres of steep land above Big Creek in Yancey County and scratched out four of those acres to grow burley tobacco. This paid the land taxes and bought the children shoes each winter. We have a family cemetery there that overlooks the creek valley and the old homeplace. Grandpa Holloway was the last schoolteacher in Lost Cove, which was abandoned in the 1930s, with the land turned over to Pisgah National Forest.

He told me everybody walked out of there together because it was too hard a living. At their house I slept under a stack of quilts in a little room off the porch. Sometimes on full-moon nights grandpa would wake me and we would let loose his coon hounds and follow them all night long. He taught me to hear the wild call of nature.

Crossing the Color Line

My arc toward social and racial justice has often meant encounters with public violence and rejection. In my strongest hour I always seem to raise the devil against me. This has happened to me as a youth, as a pastor and as a politician.

I gave my heart to the civil rights movement in 1971, sitting in a circle of rocking chairs at the Highlander Center in Tennessee. We all told our stories, over several hours' time, and how we had been affected by racism. It quickened a charge in me.

I was trained in nonviolence, hitchhiked to demonstrations in Spartanburg, Greensboro and D.C., spoke up in churches and wrote strong editorials for anybody who would publish them. I found myself in a boatload of trouble: the county sheriff came to our house to warn my daddy and the high school principal refused to process my scholarship application. A truckload of rough-looking men drove me all over Polk County one night to "educate" me about my responsibilities as a white citizen of the republic. I barely made it to graduation alive in 1972 and I have never considered moving back to Green Creek.

My father was Gurley Phillips, a decent and loving man out of Pea Ridge, North Carolina, a caretaker of many, a storyteller. He grew up between the Great Depression and the Great War, the youngest son in a sharecropping family that was dirt-poor. His father made him quit school in the 5th grade to walk 14 hours a day behind a mule. In his early 20s he took a job in a cotton mill, where he worked as a loom fixer for over 50 years. He kept a garden with a horse until he was in his 60s, and went to church every time the doors were opened. He liked to laugh and wept when he prayed in public, which he was often asked to do.

Becoming a Preacher

In the mid-1990s I was appointed the pastor of Mount Zion United Methodist Church in Pittsboro, which was one of the richest experiences of my life. It was a small congregation of mostly elders. We put a sign out at the end of the road that said "Come as You Are." I washed their feet, baptized their babies and buried their dead; in return they let me sing loudly, preach Sophia and liberation theology, and invite strange people into their presence.

During this time I developed a covenantal relationship with Elder Carrie Bolton of the United Holy Church, one of the great preachers of the South. She and I broke the color barrier in Methodist Churches throughout the region by holding joint services, with her extraordinary choir as a drawing card. At the same time I became involved in the movement for gay and lesbian inclusion in the church, meeting with other activists, pressing the message from the pulpit and offering to perform same-sex unions. These activities angered my local Board of Ordained Ministry, but it wasn't until I was elected a county commissioner that they felt threatened enough to act. I was issued an ultimatum: abandon your public office and tone down your activism or leave the pulpit.

When I refused they withdrew my appointments and revoked my scholarship to Duke Divinity School, severing me from their fellowship and support. I was kicked out of the church! From this vantage, 20 years later, I can see it as an act of grace. I loved being a pastor but I was never exclusively a Christian; I hear an old horn at daybreak and the earth religions call to me with an insistence I would have had to reconcile at great cost. At the time, however, it was heartbreaking.

Not Acting Like a White Man

In 1998 I was elected as Chatham County's first environmentalist Commissioner. It was a hard campaign and I unseated a 26-year incumbent to face an agribusiness Republican who vowed hog lagoons were so efficient that you could drink the water from their outflow. At my victory celebration. outgoing commissioner Betty Wilson offered me this prophetic statement: "Gary, I envy you so much! You don't have any enemies yet."

I led the charge to craft a strong land-use plan, which frightened the NC Homebuilders Association. After I became chair we challenged developers in open session and started a dynamic public hearing process that often filled the courthouse. We created a human relations commission. I made a bridge to the emerging Latino community, supporting dual-language programs, work equity, fair housing and access to services. I joined the Board of El Vinculo Hispano, our Latino advocacy organization. We voted down an asphalt plant supported by our Congressman and refused to permit a massive subdivision on our northern border, standing in unison to show our resolve.

My last year of office I could barely go to town without being harassed by supporters and detractors. The development lobby joined with the county conservatives and raised hundreds of thousands of dollars against my re-election,

a sum that shocked local media. A Republican business-
man switched his party affiliation to Democrat and bought
a rough cottage in my district to oppose me. Republicans
were encouraged to change their affiliation in order to vote
against me in the primary. Some did.

My opponents selected a strategy of "chipping away at
the dam," a myriad of actions designed to harm my reputa-
tion. There was a group who came to every commissioner
meeting in 2002 and asked me publicly if I was a member of
the Communist Party. I was in a time warp. "Gary Phillip's
Seat under Siege from Well-heeled Outsiders" proclaimed
the Chapel Hill Herald.

Meanwhile, I felt my center slipping from so much conflict. This is from my 2002 journal:

What about art, and the liquid sea of my life, and my
religious call? I feel flung around by unfriendly forces. I'm
spending too much time in the shallow end: information,
negotiation, facilitation, paperwork, and such shit. Maybe I
need to rip away the skin of my public life, move away from
this dry time, this dry work, this bucket of conflict and com-
peting needs that I dive into as commissioner.

One of the lowest points came when a group from the
local Ruritan Club asked me to meet with them, farmers
and mechanics and millworkers. I looked around the room
and saw my uncles, my family, the rough, fine people I had
grown up with. "Gary, we can't vote for you this time," they
said. "You just don't know how to act like a white man." Well,
I couldn't argue with that.

I lost the election by 320 votes, to great cheers and the
gnashing of teeth. The *Independent Weekly* soon ran a special feature: "Sold Out: How Developers Bought Chatham
County." Thousands upon thousands of housing lots were

approved in short order, most of which became zombie sub-
divisions during the recession and housing crash.

I could never tell my story without introducing my grand-
mothers Lily and Etta, who I carry in ceremony and who
each became the backbone and gristle of my life, imparting
in a thousand ways the wonder of the world and my place
in it. They are one of the reasons I feel at ease in working
groups of women and know how to be a true friend.

Lily Price came out of South Carolina from a family that
had high shades of several colors. She raised eight boys and
girls on nothing more than what grew out of the ground in
front of whatever farmhouse they lived in while they were
growing crops for somebody else.

After her older boys disappeared into the army and her
husband committed suicide, she settled into a trim little mobile home and lived an independent life. Luckily this was not
so far from us, and she and I were loving companions from
the time I was in diapers. We talked about everything and
she was my first true friend.

Grandma Etta could never abide being anywhere but in
her high mountains and any time she consented to visit us
she was fidgety and ready to go home in an hour or two.
I spent a large part of every summer following her around.
Etta was a forager and herbalist who had a theory of wild
"tonics" and cooked on a wood stove. She was a kind of
kitchen witch, like I am. She was a magical creature who
was brown as a berry, with hair that reached below her waist
and a quick, sure, quiet way about her. I have seen her kill a
chicken and pluck it clean before the water boiled to cook it
in. She is my reminder ghost, sitting on my shoulder with a
wry sense of humor as I go about in ceremony.

Writing and Ceremony in Service to the Wild

It's 6 AM and I have come downstairs quietly to write. Later Ilana will call me back to bed and I'll slip under the covers with a quick joy, but now I have to concentrate on Winter Solstice, when I am organizing two services, one at the new Buddhist temple and one around the bonfire at Stone Circles, my favorite social justice retreat center. We will gather to birth the sun, to affirm the lessons of the dark and welcome the light, as peoples have done for thousands of years. And one of my jobs is to prepare the wisdom teaching for Solstice.

This morning I'm inspired by the litany of all that is happening in the natural world on December 21, 2011, under our feet and above our heads and in every dark rich corner. I'm writing:

Red-winged hawks are making a harvest of first-year squirrels now that the leaf cover is down and wood chucks and eastern chipmunks have dug to their winter sleeping lairs. Noisy flocks of crows and blue-jays and robins gather at the margin of fields. Red-backed salamanders are on the move and on sudden warm days American bird grasshoppers will rise and fly. The winter forms of the Hop Merchant butterfly have drunk their last drop of the year's sun and rest in diapause. Tiny screech owls are calling from the woods on still nights and soon yearling bucks will lose their antlers.

I have not yet written about the movement of the stars (Venus in Aquarius, the night sky dominated by marching Orion) or the wintergreen on the forest floor (crane fly orchid, rattlesnake plantain, wild ginger, pipsissewa...), or even about the teeming lives under the leaf litter, but I will. It is one of my disciplines, to try to use thick description to mark the turnings of the natural world. The words I midwife spread like winter birds (brown creepers, hermit thrushes ruby-crowned kinglets, yellow-rumped warblers...), and are read at weddings, birthdays and significant public events. Sometimes I sing them and sometimes others do.

Men's Work

In the winter of 1978 I moved with a group of friends to western Massachusetts to start an intentional community. We bought a farmhouse together in Pelham and the commune prospered for years, but the most enduring legacy of that time was a men's group I helped form which has met continuously for over 30 years.

This glittering band of men meets for a full day each month, plus a five day retreat in the fall on the St. Lawrence River. I meet with them whenever possible, collaborate with them continuously, and correspond with one or more of them almost every day. We've called ourselves everything from "Men against Patriarchy" to "Men on Mushrooms." Over the years we have published a film about our group, provided childcare for women's events, organized performance art against nuclear power, participated in civil disobedience, joined together to help build an experimental solar house, and told each other our deepest personal histories over long, slow weekends. We are still a rich part of each other's lives, of each other's lifework and personal struggles. Now we are growing older and dealing with health and end of life issues: we will stay engaged until the day we help carry each other to our burying grounds.

In this lifelong process of struggle and pleasure we have become intimate with each other in a way that betrays the system of power and oppression and privilege more effectively than any one act or campaign or passionate ideal.

In a world dominated by patriarchy and its impulse for control, the fates of women and of people of color and of the earth are vulnerable to the same forces. My life's work is devoted to the enterprise of connecting an inclusive community into a web of spiritual power strong enough to stand against empire. And one of the platforms of my life continues to be this group of men: Paul Richmond, poet and performance artist; Llan Starkweather, designer/futurist; Alan Surprenant, apple farmer and anti-nuclear activist; Tom Weiner, teacher and author; Stephen Bannasch, technonerd genius for the Concord Consortium; Dick McLeester, founder of Vision Works; Stephen Trudel, counselor/men's healer and Tony Clarke, one of the world's great cabinetmakers.

The Community of Women

I am now a member of six diverse women's groups.

None of these groups started out explicitly as women's groups; three are public boards. It's just that often I find myself in a happy serious working coven of strong women, going about the restorative work of the commons, doing what needs to be done. Having called myself a womanist for over 30 years, I am now growing into the deepest incarnation of that self-description. In each of these groups I am inspired, challenged, led to responsibility and cared for.

One of my groups is a book group. We read novels and nonfiction organized around issues of social and racial justice. The conversation is an island of possibility where we take the chance to express ourselves passionately. These are strong women, graduates of a statewide leadership program, each captains of their own industry. My wife invited me to this group. Every gathering I leave feeling as if I have been showered with a fall of blessings.

I'm also part of a ritual group, a "worship committee" which gathers to plan large events marking the wheel of the year, particularly the equinoxes and solstices. We call our work "Gathering the Tribes" and our clear intention is to create a wild and safe communal open space where the seasonal, the celestial, the creative and the personal can meet and pollinate each other. On a regular basis we break bread and drink wine together, check in with each other and spend hours "chopping wood and carrying water," doing the work of our spiritual commons.

I have a plant ally group that meets monthly. We have a wide net and sometimes men actually attend this one. We are creating a seasonal calendar for the gathering of wild edibles and medicines; we share wild foods and explore the deeper narratives of plants. We eat, we talk, we work, we walk somewhere nearby and explore what's growing in our backyards and open spaces.

My public boards are Family Violence and Rape Crisis Services of Chatham County, the Abundance Foundation and the Dogwood Alliance. Of these only Dogwood has a significant percentage of men on their board. John, Neville, Rod and Daniel prove the exception to my rule that mostly it is women who show up.

Michael Meade published an article this year in *Speaking Truth to Power* titled "Where Have All the Wise Men Gone?" "We live in a time of great forgetting," he says, where precious life-sustaining elders are being replaced with just "olders who fail to recommit to the great ideals that sustain the deepest values of human life…"

I find this so true of men in general, and it is a great source of sorrow for me. On the other hand, my life is rich with women who show up over and over again with a grounded vision, the courage of conviction and the willingness to self-sacrifice—the luminous qualities of the elder.

The words of Adrienne Rich come to mind:

> My heart is moved by all I cannot save
> So much has been destroyed
> I have to cast my lot with those
> Who, age after age, perversely,
> With no extraordinary power,
> Reconstitute the world.

Joanna Macy talks about a vital arc of ceremony: We begin in gratitude (because everything must begin in gratitude), actively honor our pain for the world, open up to new ways of seeing and then commission ourselves ("sally forth," she says).

My tale follows that arc. My wish is to grow up and then grow down, like a white oak or pignut hickory or southern chestnut. In half a century, my clan, my familiars, my personal totems have moved from deer to bear to turtle to tree. I believe I am arrived at my sustainable best: standing firm, sheltering many and making mast.

May all the deities bless us in our comings and our goings. May we become indigenous. Amen.

Jessalyn Estill

Every contributor thus far has been middle aged. So introducing Jessalyn, my 26-year-old daughter, into the mix makes me wonder if young people have enough experience to bring on change. Also, Jess is in advertising in New York City. That increases my wariness of including her here.

Jess has not faced down the might of real estate developers. Nor has she stood in the face of the anti-wind lobby. And while she lacks badges such as those, she perpetually astonishes me because she "gets it." Jessalyn is one of the most resilient and persistent people I know.

As a girl Jessalyn spent part of her summers at our house in the woods of Chatham County. She left her subdivision homes in Iowa for our place in the forest, which she found strange, and filthy, and scary at times. As a young girl she found herself lost in the woods. And family lore dictates that one day while playing by herself, our family dog Chloe saved her from a "pack of wild dogs."

Jess is a New York City sophisticate. She keeps a record of her "top ten animal attacks." As a teenager she is remembered as the one who would lay down on the couch by the woodstove and proclaim, "Dad, I will do anything you want today as long as it has nothing to do with the natural world."

On the surface she is the last person I would expect to read in a book about environmental change. Yet her story is intriguing. Like so many teenagers that have gone before her, she has entered the world and found that perhaps her nutjob father was actually on to something when she was a kid.

Her strange summers in North Carolina have come to inform her thinking on sustainability and have proved an asset in her current career.

Here's my daughter Jessalyn on her role as an agent of change...

GOOD FOR SALE

Jessalyn Estill

My journey to "selling good" began two weeks after my college graduation. Armed with a degree in journalism, I moved from Columbia, Missouri to New York City. I was determined to take on the world. The year was 2008, and on the eve of economic collapse, I made the decision to take an unpaid internship at the country's first "green" advertising agency, Green Team USA.

Six months before graduating I came across Green Team in a *New York Times* article. I was captivated immediately. Here was an advertising agency using communication to better the world. Founded by a former art director and visionary, Hugh Hough, Green Team opened its doors in 1993 as an ad agency claiming, "Great Work for a Greater Cause."

Located in the heart of New York City, within an industry often perceived as exploitive, and unregulated, Green Team was a beacon of hope: a small group of people using the power of communication for causes they cared about, working to educate and empower consumers. Here was an agency in the business of selling good.

With nothing but inspiration, a metro card, and a $10 lunch stipend, I began my summer internship living in the East Village with one of my closest friends, Libby. We shared a studio apartment, and a bed, that is, until we could afford a futon. We lived off savings and graduation money. We spent the summer exchanging ideas, learning the difference between the local and express subway lines, and, thanks to generous Uncle Cameron, trying exotic foods outside our budget. This was also the summer I became a champion of the Awakening Consumer.

Green Team had identified a growing segment of the population they called the "Awakening Consumer," who were awakening to their own power in the marketplace. These were people who read newspapers, traveled the world, and engaged in their local communities. They added a new element to the purchase equation. In addition to the traditional 4 Ps of marketing (product, place, price, promotion), an Awakening Consumer adds another: purpose. These were people who considered the purpose, or the value of the brands they were buying. This group of consumers had awakened to the realization that they could bring about social and environmental change simply by voting with their dollars.

At the time, Green Team was working with Mars, Inc., to launch a good-for-you cookie (yes, really) called World Of Grains. Did the world really need another healthy snack option? Maybe not. But then again, maybe it did. If the naturally made cookie stole market share from excessively packaged and partially hydrogenated crap, well that could be a good thing. And if enough Awakening Consumers demanded the natural cookie; forcing the hydrogenated crap folks to reconsider how they make their products, well, that could be a great thing. Our job at Green Team was to raise brand awareness, and carve out a distinct and ownable space on the shelf for World Of Grains. We were working to sell a better product, working to sell something good. With the right distribution, the right messaging, and a belief in the Awakening Consumer, we could sit back and let the free market take its course.

Of course it wasn't exactly that easy. A year later, when the recession hit, Mars discontinued World of Grains and went back to focusing on its core competency; chocolate. The Mars employees working on the brand either folded into another division, or left the company. And Green Team lost a client.

I was learning the harsh reality of selling good during an economic downturn. Awakening Consumers wanted to buy better products, even more expensive products, but at what cost? Our World of Grains campaign resulted in a 150% jump in sales volume at Whole Foods Markets, and yet the brand couldn't survive.

As the summer drew to an end, and no new accounts had been landed, it quickly became painfully obvious that my time at Green Team was coming to an end. My savings account was tapped, our lease was up, and a thick layer of anxiety began to fill our non-air-conditioned studio apartment.

Determined to stay in the city, I frantically began applying for jobs, and looking for work in the interim. Libby and I also began the hunt for a new place to live, which ultimately meant spending hours, days, weeks on Craigslist, only to find that the "MUST SEE!!! REAL 2br NO FEE**" place in midtown was actually a railroad (you had to walk through one bedroom to get to the other) with a 12% broker fee, to be paid to a "broker" we hadn't hired.

It didn't take long to become familiar with the NY real estate scene. We had the realty office numbers saved in our phones. We were on a first name basis with most of the Hasidic Jewish brokers in Brooklyn. And most importantly, we had developed a solid list of questions to ask before making the trip to see an apartment.

"When you say two bedrooms, do you mean there are actual walls, or would we need to buy a wall?"

"Is the only bathroom in one of the bedrooms?"

"The ad says, 'Charming Upper West Side location', do you really mean Harlem?"

Eventually we landed a one bedroom on the Upper East Side. We rented a wall with a door, converting the space into a two bedroom apartment that would be our home for the next two years.

On my mother's first visit, she remarked that the hallway of our building looked like something out of *Law & Order: Special Victims Unit*. But the inside was cozy, filled with matching Ikea decor, and the occasional piece of street furniture that was just too cute to leave on the curb. I was proud of how far we'd come from the days of the futon. So was my mother.

During the early days of our first New York apartment, Libby landed a financial reporter position, and I got a waitressing job at a trendy restaurant in Greenwich Village. Instead of selling good, I was selling whatever I could to make rent. At this point, it was griddle-cooked pizzas and homemade gelato.

Continuing my "real" job search on days off from the restaurant was a challenge. At the time, Green Team was unique in specializing in social and environmentally responsible brands. I wanted to stay in communications, but selling myself as someone who had spent the last three months learning how to sell good wasn't working. Selling myself as someone who had just completed an internship at an advertising agency did.

After several interviews, I was offered a job at a full service healthcare communications agency, to work as an account coordinator for an anti-depressant drug. The money was good; starting pay was well above the average account coordinator position. The offer was good; full benefits including a matching 401k plan. The promise was good; I was assured promotions were frequent and it would be easy to rise to the top.

The problem was the industry. I have long considered the prescription drug industry to have an abusive relationship with the media. To be clear, I have a great respect for the advancements of treatments in the long-neglected field of mental health. But the thought of actively encouraging people to "ask their doctor" about the latest money-making drug for a disorder you may or may not have was deeply unsettling. This would be a far departure from where I wanted to be, and where I had been headed at Green Team. Then again, pulling 12 hour shifts at a restaurant 45 minutes from my apartment wasn't the New York life I imagined either.

Two days after I was offered the position, Green Team's director of client services, Milton Kapelus called. Milton wanted to know if I had a job. If not, Milton said, in his charming South African accent, "We want you back at

Green Team." I was ecstatic. The pay wasn't great, and the company wouldn't be able to match a 401k, but the decision was clear. Without hesitation I made the choice to begin my full-time career selling good. I believed I could work to harness the power of business to better the world, and I was determined to prove it.

I decided to keep my waitressing job for extra cash after being hired at Green Team. I was required to work three shifts a week at the restaurant, which meant a double on Saturday (10:00 AM to 12:30 PM) and the brunch shift on Sunday. The work was grueling. Waiting tables in New York City is by far the most difficult job I have ever had. The pace was intense, and the hours exhausting. Not to mention my Italian pronunciation of the menu items was poor at best, and my knowledge of cheese regions practically nonexistent.

I was miserable, but I needed the money. I had been living with a blowup air mattress in our new apartment and was saving money for a bed. The air mattress wasn't so bad, but it had a small hole in it. So, every morning around 4:00 AM, after sinking into the floor, Libby would hear the screeching noise of my mattress being plugged in and blown back up again. I wasn't quitting my restaurant job until I bought a real bed—box spring and everything.

Juggling my new career at Green Team and weekends at the restaurant was nearly impossible. It wasn't long before my manager pulled me aside after I had missed yet another server wine-tasting class, to tell me that my services would no longer be needed. I was devastated and humiliated. It was the first and only job I had ever been fired from.

But I had Green Team. I was excited to get up in the morning and I enjoyed staying late. At lunchtime, when the staff would eat together in the communal kitchen, I'd pull out a PB&J sandwich and engage in conversations about gay marriage, religion, new art exhibits, pop culture, healthcare. I was part of a team, a small group of fifteen people from all over the world who had come together to make a difference. So what if I didn't have a bed? I had field trips to the Native American Museum on Columbus Day. I had a campaign to help protect the world's oceans. I had a video project on the concept of energy. Most of all I had passion. I was working to make a difference in consumerism, and selling good felt great.

As an account coordinator at Green Team I worked primarily on the agency's travel accounts. In many cases, the travel clients were not interested in sustainability. To most tourism boards, sustainability means keeping the economy stimulated by sustaining the same number of travelers each year.

Yet travel had always been part of Green Team's DNA. Green Team's first client was in fact a destination—the principality of Monaco. And the concept of sustainable travel was slowly gaining traction. In addition to VisitBritian and Monaco, the roster of travel accounts included pioneers of the movement like Lindblad Expeditions, and countries committed to preserving their destinations, like Ecuador. More and more tourism boards began to see the value in protecting the destinations they worked to promote.

Collectively we wrestled with representing clients that fell short on environmental responsibility but maintained that the more one saw of the world, the more one would care about protecting it. Experiencing the world responsibly was something good worth selling. Truth be told, the travel accounts also helped the agency keep its doors open, allowing Green Team to continue the "greater cause" work.

My first "greater cause" account was the Biodiversity Project, a nonprofit organization hired by the Mississippi River Network to encourage action to keep the Mississippi healthy. Serving as a critical habitat to over 400 species of wildlife, and providing drinking water to 18 million people, the abuse of the Mississippi River could no longer be ignored.

Green Team had been hired to develop a campaign in the ten Mississippi River states to inspire the public, policymakers, and the agricultural community to restore and protect its own lifeline. The campaign was called "1 Mississippi." It was a rallying cry to citizens in the area, reminding them how much they counted on the river, and asking them if the river could count on them.

I loved the project. The people were passionate, the cause was important, and the strategy brilliant. Did I believe our 1 Mississippi campaign was going to force local farmers to more closely monitor their nutrient runoff? Maybe not. But I did believe the campaign could spark a conversation and that we had equipped the Biodiversity Project with the right communication tools to develop and sustain a grassroots movement.

Those in the nonprofit world know all too well that funding is tight, especially for communications efforts. And those in the communications industry know that when times are tough, ad budgets, and marketing efforts, are the first to go. It came as no surprise that when the economy tanked, our nonprofit clients were the first to go. Some of our corporate projects followed suit all too quickly. Even our lucrative travel accounts began to panic and scale back their budgets. Our sources of revenue, and client prospects quickly began to evaporate.

Of course Green Team was not alone during this time. The global economic storm forced many sustainable communication organizations to make sacrifices, or shut down completely. *Plenty Magazine*, a bimonthly publication dedicated to "giving a voice to the green revolution," closed down in 2009 after four years. Other publications and startups working to sell good also collapsed, and as the recession went on, the loss of green jobs in the media industry grew more and more worrisome. Could those of us trying to sell a better world sustain ourselves during crunch time?

The shrinking client roster certainly took its toll on the agency. One by one members of the team were let go. It wasn't long before I was called into Hugh's office and told I would be cut down to part-time beginning immediately. I was terrified. I was only seven months into my lease and barely making it each month on a full salary. I had just started my big New York adventure. Had I already failed? I called my dad.

"Well darling, I don't know what to tell you. It's 1929 and you moved to Manhattan."

My father went on to explain that this partial layoff was really a "gift basket" of healing and growth. Green Team would survive, or it wouldn't. I could choose to stay, and continue to learn how to sell good, or I could choose to jump from what could turn out to be a sinking ship.

I chose to stay. Libby and I bought cheap champagne, declared it "National Gift Basket Day," and I began to look for a part-time job.

After two weeks working as a hostess at a local bakery, the owner decided there wasn't enough business to have a hostess on staff. I was paid in cash, and sent back to square one. I then applied for a part-time nanny position on Sittercity.com. The hours were flexible, the pay was decent, and after a $10 background check and an in-person interview with both the parents and the children, I was hired.

The family had two children, both in elementary school. After working at Green Team in the morning, I would pick the children up from school on the Upper West Side, and take them to their apartment on the Upper East side. I would watch them while their mother ran errands in the afternoon.

My stint as a nanny would later give me a new perspective on children raised in Manhattan. There was no yard, so the kids went to Central Park. There was no real neighborhood of kids, so play dates involved coordination among drivers. Class field trips meant visiting the Whitney, and the Natural History Museum. These were children with access to world class culture, and yet no understanding of pickup street hockey, or neighborhood-wide hide-and-go-seek.

I kept my part-time nanny job a secret from most of my friends and family. I didn't know how to explain that I had turned down a high-paying Big Pharma job only to end up a part-time world-saver, part-time nanny. As the weeks went on, I began to question what I was doing in New York, and in the advertising industry at all. Still, I clung to the belief that communication was the answer; that selling good could change consumer behavior and business practices.

My time with the Manhattan family finally came to an end when Green Team offered me a full-time account executive position, three months after being cut down to part-time. I would no longer be assisting on various projects, but was instead asked to manage two accounts full time. I was back. The team had been pared down, but the agency had weathered the storm.

I too, had weathered the most difficult time in my New York life. Now more than ever I was confident in my career, and after two incredible years on the Upper East Side, I had moved to the West Village with the love of my life, Dan. I spent the week using communication to advance society, and my weekends with Dan, exploring the winding streets and tiny restaurants of the village, picnicking along the Hudson River, and planning our future together.

Dan supported my long hours at the agency and, as time went on, Green Team slowly began to recover. The years ahead brought opportunities to work with larger NGOs such as National Geographic and National Audubon Society, and brands such as Johnson & Johnson. I grew as a leader on the account team, and was given more and more responsibility and opportunities. I quickly became the account Supervisor for VisitScotland, and the editor-in-chief of *g-Think*, the agency's quarterly newsletter.

Still, even in 2011, the pain of the recession still lingered, and Green Team was faced with an even larger issue. Sustainable communications was no longer niche. Suddenly we weren't the only ones out there selling good, and our competition included traditional agencies that suddenly claimed to have a "green" division.

The sentiment at Green Team was that these large agencies had randomly assigned employees with no real sustainability experience to become part of their new green divisions. We knew those other agencies didn't have the same heart or experience in selling good, and yet they had the gravitas to win the same pitches and accounts we were going after.

The reality was the world had caught up to Green Team. We may have been the first in the realm of advertising to use our powers for good, but we were far from the last. It was the big "Madison Avenue" agencies of the world who threatened to leave Green Team in the dust, a mere bystander to a movement we had helped shape 20 years earlier.

In 2011, Green Team decided to refocus its message. Refocusing meant a new website, a new mission statement, a new "elevator pitch." It also meant making difficult decisions about existing clients. In the fall of 2011, Green Team decided not to re-pitch Puerto Vallarta, a six-year account that no longer fit within the agency's mission. Ending our relationship with Puerto Vallarta was a risk; it meant walking away from a steady monthly income, and possibly downsizing the creative staff in order to focus on our core competency of sustainability.

The goal was to hone our message, to target larger NGOs and brands, with larger budgets. We began to move further and further away from traditional advertising and media, and more into brand positioning, and what we called "Purpose Branding."

The rebranding of the agency was an effort to more clearly communicate to businesses what we had always believed: a product that has a higher purpose, other than selling itself, will sell more products. We would continue to sell good, to use the power of communications, but we needed to reframe our message, to become more relevant to businesses' bottom lines.

A year later, as I write this, only time will tell if Green Team's renewed positioning can keep the agency relevant. But I still believe. After years of shared futons and non-airconditioned apartments, of odd jobs and career achievements, of falling in love with a city and falling in love with my husband, I find myself with an unwavering resolve and a true optimism for tomorrow.

Communication can change the world. And those of us using this great power for the greater good, those of us dedicated to selling good will continue to act as powerful agents of change.

Eric Henry

I first met Eric when he needed some methanol for his homebrew biodiesel operation. He drove to Summer Shop at my house, and we hand rolled fifty-five gallons of methanol from my drum to his. I'm not sure I charged him for it—and he has been grateful ever since.

Eric grabs onto dreams and does not let go. My favorite is his "Cotton of the Carolinas" project in which he goes from "dirt to shirt" right here in North Carolina. When he embarked on producing organic cotton they said it could not be done. He found some cotton farmers and convinced them to give it a try. When the organic cotton out-performed the conventional varieties it commanded such a high price in the market that Eric needed to borrow money to stay in the game. He arranged a Slow Money loan that I participated in as a lender.

At the loan closing, Eric's business partner, Tom Sineath, commented on how "Eric does not take 'no' for an answer."

Tom gave a brief speech about Eric's tenacity, and doggedness in the face of adversity.

Tom, incidentally, is no slouch on the sustainability front. He's the practical one in their partnership. He's the backseat logistics guy, who helps make Eric's visions come to pass. And he's an inventor. He has a deep understanding of "how things work." From finance to physics, Tom is the guy that every sustainability prize fighter would want in their corner.

Sometimes at Piedmont Biofuels I try to get dispatched to deliver fuel to Burlington so that I can stop in and talk to Tom. Eric is never around. He is constantly on the road. But Tom is always happy to interrupt his day to talk to me about whatever he is working on. Sometimes it's his solar powered automated gate for their chicken coop. Sometimes it's about bank financing. Whenever I get to spend some time with Tom at TS Designs, it's a good day on the fuel truck.

A lot of my relationship with Eric has been formed in the "public sphere." We don't hang out socially together, but we frequently find ourselves on stage with one another. We have shared the limelight from Durham, North Carolina at a "Fourth Sector" conference, to Charleston, South Carolina at a Business Alliance for Local Living Economies (BALLE) conference. Since much of our relationship has been formed in the public eye, we have developed a friendly banter about one another.

I think we follow him on our project. He says he is trying to keep up with us. He's only one county away from us, and it is hard to tell who is in the shadow of who.

If I were to run the ledger, biodiesel would go in my column. Employment would go in his. Solar electric started in my column when I put up a 2K array. Eric then trumped it with an 8K unit. Michael Tiemann and I then took it back with a 96K solar double cropping project. Compost would go to Eric, as would micro wind. I would claim the sustainable agriculture point. And he would concede that his vision for Company Shops, the new coop grocery story in Burlington was inspired in part by Chatham Marketplace in Pittsboro. And on and on it goes.

Ours is a good-natured and productive competition.

My path has crossed with Eric's for over a decade. On the surface our relationship is entirely "business," but occasionally it crosses into the "personal" space.

One night at a bar called the Eddy in Saxapahaw, there was a convening of the "New North Carolina Economy." Eric spoke. I spoke. Everybody spoke. I ate and drank with impunity, and when I took a cell call from my daughter, I mistakenly drove home without paying. Eric picked up my tab.

For a couple of guys who barely know one another, Eric and I have become deeply entangled. Sometimes I vacuum vegetable oil out of his yard. Sometimes he shows up at the plant to take a workshop, or for lunch. Sometimes we light out together, to avoid the glare of an audience, to exchange ideas in a back booth of a café.

Here's Eric's story. He writes like he lives: with great passion and intensity...

THE JOURNEY

Eric Henry

Perhaps when considering the concept of the glass half empty as being the glass half full, I'm one of those people who will ask why we need the glass in the first place, or even what material the glass is made of. As far back as I can remember, I have tried to be aware of my surroundings and to find ways to improve or minimize my impact on the earth. I am still not sure what drives me in this direction, but I do know that I live for the moment, and it doesn't take much to get me to change course.

I am not sure why I started an organic garden in my parent's backyard while growing up in downtown Burlington, North Carolina. I am not sure why I started buying CFL light bulbs (Panasonic, Made in Japan) 25 years ago when the cost was $20 per bulb. Twenty years ago, I nudged our employees to stop using Styrofoam cups by requiring that they start using their own coffee mugs. I am not sure why I started making biodiesel almost ten years ago when diesel fuel cost $1 per gallon.

I can't tell you why our company started making t-shirts in North Carolina nearly six years ago when most apparel manufacturing companies were still moving offshore to pursue cheaper labor. And I have no idea how I convinced my business partner to invest $70,000 in a solar array when our company still owed us thousands in personal loans.

I'm not sure why I helped open a co-op grocery store in downtown Burlington when all other retail had moved to the outlying shopping centers—our community of 150,000 people currently supports three super Walmart stores.

Clearly, I cannot connect or remember anything specifically in my life that put me on this path. Maybe I was looking for something beyond profit and money.

I grew up in a middle-class family in a middle-class neighborhood in Burlington, North Carolina. My dad was the assistant transportation manager for Burlington Industries, which at the time was one of the biggest textile companies in the United States. Unfortunately, the demise of Burlington Industries came courtesy of the North American Free Trade Agreement (NAFTA).

One of my first memories of taking an environmental stance was in the late 60s. I was about ten years old, and I refused to ride in my dad's Opal that was burning some serious motor oil. I lost that battle, and I do not remember why I was so concerned about the gray-blue smoke coming out of the exhaust pipe, but no one else at the time seemed to care about it or my protest.

Remember, these were the days when it was ok to throw your trash out the car window or dump the used motor oil from your car behind the house. There was a creek in front and down the block from our house that I played in quite a bit—I remember multicolored water and soap suds, and I remember that the water would periodically start killing the crayfish and frogs routinely each summer. For some reason, people accepted this dying of creatures without questioning the pollution.

In my early teen years, I put a vegetable garden in our back yard, and I implemented practices I read about in Rodale's *Organic Gardening* magazine. Instead of the preferred pest killer Sevin dust, which was presented as the miracle death powder by my family and friends, I sought alternative healthier solutions.

That garden led me to build a geodesic greenhouse so I could start my own seeds and grow tomatoes in the winter. My grandfather helped. I also started food-waste collection at the pizza restaurant where I worked, and this led me to enter North Carolina State University with an interest in agriculture. No one in my family had been involved in farming, nor had any interest in pursuing it. Now, almost 40 years later, my wife and I have bought a small farm with a double purpose: managing her love of horses and allowing me to get my hands back in the dirt.

While in high school I moved off the path as cars, girls, and the ability to purchase alcohol while still underage distracted me. But I seemed to get back on track when I left for college and started to learn about Earth Day celebrations. It was around this time that the t-shirt business started to evolve, and my business partner at TS Designs thinks a lot of my drive and vision galvanized during the tenth anniversary of Earth Day in 1980.

For over 30 years, I have been the president of TS Designs. I helped grow our business to over 100 employees only to see it destroyed in the mid-90s by NAFTA. I traded in my BMW and country club membership for a biodiesel burning VW and a major investment in a co-op grocery store.

I quickly learned the power of money when the customers and relationships that took me years to build were completely put aside because someone in some place outside the United States would do the work cheaper. I saw the American consumer get swept up with cheaper prices while not observing or caring where the clothes they wore were made. I was forced to lay off a lot of people, saw friends shutting down their businesses and communities completely destroyed—all for the sake of cheaper prices.

It took a few years for us to find a new direction for TS Designs, and it was my friend Sam Moore that introduced us to the idea of a triple bottom line.

Today, as we look at record high unemployment and an economy stuck in neutral, I hope that I can stay in the game long enough to see this situation turn around by bringing back jobs to the United States. Meanwhile, we're doing our part by ensuring TS Designs' clothes are made down the street, not half way around the world.

Over the years as we've incorporated the triple-P model (people, planet, profits), TS Designs has become the melting pot in our community for sustainable ideas and a gathering place for like-minded folks that are interested in a more sustainable future. Recently, we have started hosting monthly tours and helped our local community college to launch a green curriculum.

I have found it takes a community to move these many projects and ideas ahead. Part of my learning curve with people has been once they realize we have a business that has a vision and purpose beyond just lining our wallets, they want to become a part of that vision, and begin offering their help. From our garden, to beehives, to renewable energy— we have so many friends that want to assist and participate.

The Profit side of the triple bottom line has always been the hardest to obtain. After NAFTA, it took us to 2008 before we had a business running again on all three cylinders. Our excitement was short-lived courtesy of the destruction created by the economic meltdown in 2009. The current recession only pushes me harder to find a way to make the triple bottom line business approach work for the apparel industry.

Most of the t-shirts we offer at TS Designs are made in the USA, but the majority of our shirts are made right here in North Carolina. Taking a page from the local food movement, we focused on the fact that our state is usually the third or fourth largest grower of conventional cotton in the USA. With this knowledge, we began looking for ways to connect our finished product directly to farmers in our state, and launched our new brand, "Cotton of the Carolinas."

Typically, a t-shirt in your local big box store can travel 13,000 miles from production to the store shelves. Not our Cotton of the Carolinas shirts. Our "dirt to shirt" concept means a shirt travels just 700 miles—all in North Carolina— with a completely transparent supply chain.

Encouraged by the success of that brand, we began to work directly with farmers to launch the growing and harvesting of the first certified organic cotton in North Carolina in the summer of 2011—something we were told could never be done. We are now on the verge of making the world's most sustainable t-shirt—local, transparent, organic and produced using the greenest processes. We hope that this will connect jobs and the environment, proving that this is a crucial relationship, and that we really have no other sustainable choice.

Throughout my journey, I have learned it takes a community. There are so many things that are broken in our society—overuse of fossil fuels, industrial agriculture and blind consumerism, to name just a few. It's difficult to stay on top of these topics as well as other areas that impact my day to day living, and that's when I turn to my friends and community of different experts to guide me along. I think this is what has made the journey the most enjoyable:, all the great people I have met along the way who have a passion for life rather than just a quest for a fat checkbook.

Not to say this journey's been easy—at times it's been tough and caused a lot of pain and sacrifice, especially for my wife, who has been one of my biggest supporters over our 26 years of marriage. It has been a frustrating journey in that most of my business life I've always had to try to make the dollars work with my passion in order to do my small part to make the world a better place.

Slowly, I am starting to see a few things starting to turn, but I still sometimes wonder, can we turn the car around quickly enough before it goes flying off the cliff? It's so frustrating that we still have to validate the very real concepts of peak oil and climate change to some groups. But, the power of community is so much greater than the voice of a few, and for the most part, I am very hopeful we can turn this around...but then again, I see that glass as being half full.

Sustainability is a journey, not a destination.

Megan Toben

Megan Toben is dangerously seductive. When you are in her presence it is best to be completely clear about your own ideas. Otherwise her enthusiasms will overwhelm you.

My relationship to Megan, and Pickards Mountain, started from afar. Our interns would leave our project and travel up the mountain to hang out. I had never made the trek, but stories would make it back to me.

We were making biodiesel. They were making biodiesel. Yawn. They were growing pigs and chickens for meat. Interesting. They had massive potluck dinners with circle conversations around the wood fire. Interesting. Someone told me their fireplace was bigger than my house.

For years I heard about Megan at Pickards Mountain, but I had never met her, and I had never been there to see the place. Her Eco Institute has often been held up as a project that is similar to—and often much better than—what we offer at Piedmont.

When I finally made the journey to the top of the mountain, I was as amazed as everyone who visits. They had a fascinating collection of yurts and domes and yomes for their intern housing that made me jealous.

The place was simply fabulous.

I believe my first trip there was to a political fundraiser. And once I was familiar with the place, I started returning frequently. When their biodiesel project was closed down, I started delivering fuel to their storage tank. I attended one of their Awakening the Dreamer workshops.

I became a customer of Megan's pastured pork. I would fill up a box with chops and sausage and hams, and I would randomly deliver them to friends on my way home.

Our relationship broadened—from threatening competitor to fellow islander—and our friendship deepened.

One day I was sitting with Megan on their expansive back porch, looking out on Chapel Hill below, and she announced that she was simply too tired to continue. She was going to give it all up, move into a little house at the bottom of the mountain and simply raise her two young children. She was done pushing sustainability up the hill every day.

Her exhaustion had a profound impact on me. The next morning I described her state to Tami. "We are hiding Jews," I said. "When you are hiding Jews you can't simply give up because you are tired.

"The culture is against us. Our institutions, our media, our politicians, our economy, everything we know is about cheap reliable energy even if we have to rip the top off a mountain or spill into the Gulf of Mexico. When it comes to energy our culture is ready to sew a yellow star onto the coat of anyone looking for wholesale change."

"You can't use that expression," said Tami. "That's too inflammatory."

I thought about it all morning, and by midday I had changed my tune. I had lunch with Maria Kingery, one of the founders of Southern Energy Management. I explained to her about Megan's exhaustion, and I explained how instead of "hiding Jews" we are all part of the resistance.

Maria looked at me and said, "Part of the resistance? I just gave a speech at the Sustainable Jobs Fund conference last week and I quoted you," she said. "I said 'there is enough for everyone and that you get everything you want or something better.'"

She shook her head. "You can't tell me everything is abundant one moment and that we are part of the resistance the next."

By the end of the day I had switched the analogy to "life boats." Megan runs one at Pickards Mountain. I run one at Piedmont.

I'm not sure what the best analogy is—but here is Megan's story in her words…

PICKARDS
MOUNTAIN ECO INSTITUTE

Megan Toben

I was engaged to marry. We were signed up to join the Peace Corps in Central America.

My perspective as an undergraduate Biology major at Elon University left me with a sense of despair and urgency. Global climate change, drastic deforestation and habitat loss, unprecedented species extinction rates, air and water toxicity, wars over scarce resources, overpopulation, and the social implications of the industrial growth society felt like an unstoppable avalanche of catastrophe.

I wanted to help. I wanted to get my hands dirty. I wanted to climb trees and plant seeds. I wanted to understand, from the ground up, how we humans had gotten ourselves into this mess.

I knew I had to escape the industrial society, the house of cards, built on finite resources and dependent on infinite growth.

My classmates wanted to find a cure for cancer. I wanted to find a cure for humanity.

I couldn't ignore the striking similarities between the epidemics of uncontrolled growth in our bodies and in our world.

Who are we? What are we doing?

What purpose were we meant to serve in this Earth Community? My intuition told me that we had known a better way at some point in human history. There were ancient cultures who had understood our place in the sacred web of life. But we Americans had forgotten.

We had deviated so far as to isolate ourselves in ivory towers and sterile laboratories to perform the "study of life."

I began to search for the truth in places where traces of traditional cultures still remained.

I heard stories of a "good witch" who lived on a magical farm with a giant treehouse. I knew I had to find her.

Carolyn was almost 70 years old, but as soon as our eyes met, I knew.

After a series of walks in the woods, I cancelled the wedding. I abandoned the Peace Corps.

My soul, parched from sterile biology laboratories, thirsted for her wild wise-woman ways. I followed her around. I made muffins in order to have an excuse to visit her. I lapped up her words. Her ideas, her way of thinking, were like salve to very deep, old wounds.

I volunteered to help with educational programs at her nonprofit, The Center for Education, Imagination, and the Natural World at Timberlake Farm. I fell in love with her land and the children who came. The children likewise fell in love with the land, and that was wonderful to witness.

I learned that much of Carolyn's perspective came from her teacher and friend, Thomas Berry, cultural historian and eco-theologian.

Thomas writes that instead of being a malignant presence on Earth, we must learn to become a benign—or even better, a mutually enhancing part of the Earth Community.

I began to understand, through his ideas, that the empirical perspective I had honed during my undergraduate years was precisely what was allowing us to pretend that humans are separate from "nature." The notion of "saving the environment" was lovely, but the general assumption was that we would survive independent of the rest of the Earth Community.

I came out the other side of my own intense religious exploration aghast at the great separation that the church had promulgated. Our understanding of heaven as separate and apart leaves Earth as waiting room, supply closet, and trashcan. This seemingly harmless assumption, when multiplied by billions of humans with free choice, has left the beautiful and complex systems of Earth in shambles. For the first time in human history, all life is threatened.

Then came Tim. One morning, after a curiously wonderful encounter with her son, Carolyn held me by the shoulders, looked me in the eyes and said "You should marry my son." We had met at a Thomas Berry Lecture and made a bonfire together afterwards.

At first I laughed, flattered and amused. Then, I walked in the woods with him.

I found a man who shared my deep love for Mother Earth, and my despair over her plight. We stopped to stroke soft mossy patches and watch hawks circle overhead. I cried on his shoulder about toxins in the air and waters. Together we rejoiced over the sheer beauty of life, and mourned the losses of species and cultures. In each other we found glimpses of our deepest and most true selves, and together we found our path. It wasn't well-marked, had lots of rocks and knobby roots, and it didn't seem like many had walked it before.

Tim and I fell in love while exploring the forests, meadows and streams of his land, called Pickards Mountain. On my 22nd birthday, we built a garden and planted our first seeds. We began to learn the names of the plants and animals who shared the land with us.

People who shared our compassion for the crisis came to potluck dinners on Wednesday nights. A wind turbine and solar array were erected to provide clean energy. Composting toilets saved fresh water. A little space in the barn provided a home for a small co-op of folks who made Biodiesel fuel out of vegetable grease. A beautiful chicken coop held a flock of 20 hens who gave delicious eggs with deep orange yolks. Friends, hungry for simple living, asked if they could camp in our woods. Some stayed for a long time. We made explanations to neighbors and invited them to join us for farm suppers. Over long conversations, we discovered they shared our concerns for the world.

I received phone calls and emails from people curious about our projects. We began hosting educational programs and field trips and called our work "Pickards Mountain Eco-Institute." The name always felt a bit presumptuous to me, like we knew the answers, but Tim convinced me that we wouldn't be taken seriously if we called it "Pickards Mountain Center for Loving the Earth, Healing the World, Making Peace, Living in the Woods, Growing Food, Holding

Hands in Circles and Learning Together." (Plus, we weren't trying to come off as a commune.)

So, Pickards Mountain Eco-Institute was born. UNC-Chapel Hill asked us to be one of their Triangle Sustainability Field Study Sites. The Abundance Foundation invited us to share their 501(c)3 nonprofit status. We hosted classes from over 40 local schools who watched the wind turbine turn, learned about biofuels, pulled and ate organic carrots, and asked questions about the future of life on Earth.

We signed up as a host site with the international organization Worldwide Opportunities on Organic Farms (WWOOF) Members, usually recent college graduates restless to see and save the world, sign up to help on farms in exchange for room and board. People came from all over the country, and a few from outside the US. We met people on many different journeys, invited them into our daily lives, and learned from each other.

We've probably had two hundred WWOOFers over five years. Some only stayed a night, but some stayed almost a year and became integral to farm life. The garden kept them busy with pulling weeds, watering, and harvesting vegetables. They fed and fell in love with the chickens, pigs, goats and ducks. Someone taught us to dry herbs and make baskets. We read and talked about the state of the world. Around evening bonfires, we listened to stories of their adventures and songs they had learned along the way. We shared ideas of the latest sustainability techniques, most of which were resurrections of ancient methods or technologies based on natural systems. Sometimes their dogs would attack chickens or they would accidentally almost set fire to the woods, but mostly it was a mutually enhancing experience.

We invited inspirational teachers to host workshops in herbalism, wild foods, holistic medicine, wild mushrooms, permaculture, simple living, growing food, cultivating mushrooms and the Transition Town movement .

I always invited WWOOFers and interns to attend workshops, tag along with field trips and join community potluck dinners. Our potluck group grew, until there were sometimes 100 people in our circle. Many of them were new faces, and I was always amazed at the relationships and realizations that emerged. There were doctors and lawyers, teachers, students, vagabonds, clergy, anarchists, legislators, engineers, entrepreneurs, and their families. People in ties would sit next to people with dreadlocks, and end up chatting about politics and eggplant. Tim and I loved it. Local schoolteachers found great fodder for classroom discussions. Families asked questions about rooftop solar and hired local contractors to install systems. People tasted baba ganoush, red pepper hummus, and nettle pesto. Many said they were the most delicious meals they had eaten. Kids chased chickens, fed goats and played in the sand beneath the shade of the solar array. At least three couples fell in love on the land and eventually married.

I felt incredibly fulfilled. Our first child, Kaia Maathai Toben, was born in August of 2005. She was named after Nobel Peace Laureate Wangari Maathai who started the Greenbelt Movement in Kenya, and was christened by Thomas Berry. Kaia rode on my back while I farmed and taught.

Margaret Krome-Lukens came into our lives just in time to save me and the farm from falling apart. Deep dedication to my new role as mama was teaching me about my limits

as a human being. I couldn't do it all. Margaret had the in-
fectious optimism of sunshine and the self-disciplined work
ethic of a ninja. We found ourselves in a beautiful partnership, taking care of the farm together.

Margaret and I both loved the way the schoolchildren
came alive on the farm. The look on parents' faces when their
children reached for, picked and ate green beans and tomatoes from the vine was priceless. We also loved the way children immediately saw the wisdom and beauty in working
with nature. Why wouldn't we get all our energy from clean
sources like the sun and the wind?

Once, a little boy in the first grade visited on a field trip
with his class. He sat quietly listening to our explanation
of the solar energy system. His brow furrowed as he ex-
amined the huge panels. "Where does the energy come in?
And where does it go out?" Then, later, as his teacher had
requested, we were exploring the way plants catch energy
from the sun and turn it into what they need to grow. We
were imagining together that our bodies were plants. Our
feet were the roots growing down into the soil, our arms the
branches, our faces the flowers. As we reached our hands/
leaves up to the sun, this little boy jumped up and yelled "A
plant is like a SOLAR PANEL!"

Children's curiosity and thirst for knowledge come from
their inborn love for the natural world. One of the greatest
gifts we can give them is time outdoors to explore and wonder. The heartbreaking times are when children have been
denied these opportunities and disconnected from that love
by fear. I will never forget a group of girls from a Greensboro
inner city school who simply would not step off of the gravel.
They clung to one another, shrieking about dogs, spiders,

and snakes. When, finally, by the end of the day, these girls were sitting in the grass describing bird songs they heard and loved, I felt like the morning had been a success.

This work is not about giving people all the answers—we don't have all the answers to give. But we know how to listen for good clues. And one of them is the knowledge that we don't come into this world afraid. We come into this world curious and amazed. We come into this world believing we can talk to animals, and that trees deserve to be climbed and hugged.

One day, a middle school ESL (English as a Second Language) class came on a field trip from Durham. When the teacher first contacted us about the class, I assured her that I was comfortable with conversational Spanish, and my wonderful co-leader Margaret with conversational French. She responded that her 30 students, mostly from Southeast Asia and Africa, spoke 12 languages, not including local dialects. She assured me that they would "mostly" understand my English.

The students were afraid to get off of the bus. The teacher had warned me that some of these kids had been through serious life trauma like abuse and refugee camps. Once we coaxed them off the bus and into a circle, the next task was getting them to speak their names. The teacher helped, and repeated the names, many of which were new to us. I began to explain that Pickards Mountain was about learning to meet our needs in ways that were healthy and good for the Earth. We knew that the air and waters were being poisoned by industrial processes, and that people were acting without respect for the natural systems and other living beings. We were trying to change that.

They looked at me with huge eyes and guarded expressions. I have no idea if they understood a word I said. Eventually, I gave up on talking and walked them over to the rabbit hutch. Since rabbits are prey animals, every time they get lifted off the ground they think they are getting eaten. As I sat down with this scared rabbit in my lap, and motioned for the students to come closer, I didn't know who was more afraid. One shaky hand reached out to stroke the rabbit's fur, then another. I thought I saw a little smile.

Our next stop was the greenhouse. I picked a few leaves, tasting them and passing them around to share. I wasn't using many words, except maybe the names of the plants. I started to notice sounds of recognition, and realized the students were naming the plants in their own languages. I will never forget the excitement one African girl expressed over the beets. She summoned up the words "We have this in my country!" She hadn't yet seen them in the US, and was so thrilled, I gave her an armload to take to her family. The taste of the beets had taken her back to a time and a place when her life had roots.

I've gotten used to kids falling in love with our two playful farm dogs, but one small boy from Burma couldn't leave them alone. He played with them, wrestled with them, and hugged them. At the end of the day, I noticed him telling his teacher about how he used to take care of the dogs in his village. She later told me that was the most English he had spoken all year.

A group of high school students visited Pickards Mountain one spring from a school in Raleigh. At their teacher's request, we created a three-day program for them. When they arrived, a kid named Jake caught my eye. With his multiple piercings, henna tattoos, and shaggy blue hair, he was hard to miss. My first impression was that he wasn't so excited about the field trip.

The first day we talked about their current understanding of the state of things, learned their names, and gave them a tour of the farm and projects.

The next day, we put them to work in the garden and on the cob building project. They learned the basics of planting and harvesting, soil testing, irrigation and natural building.

On the third day, we explored the details of the environmental crisis, using a framework created by the Pachamama Alliance (pachamama.org).

Where are we?

How did we get here?

What is possible for the future?

Where do we go from here?

We witnessed a beautiful shift in consciousness over these three days. After they left, I got an email from Jake, the blue haired kid. It read, "Thank you for allowing me to visit Pickards Mountain Eco-Institute. I now know who I want to be and what I want to do with my life."

Jake spent much of that summer camping out on the farm and collaborating on a cob cottage. At the end of the summer, he was indeed a new version of himself. His parents credited our work together for his successful graduation from high school and his passionate pursuit of further education.

Tim was invited to Iceland on a fishing trip with Bill McDonough, one of the world's leading green architects. Together they dreamed up a groundbreaking green building project for Chapel Hill.

Tim purchased a portion of a block in downtown Chapel Hill. The few buildings on it were condemned, and the soil laced with trash and leaked toxins. I watched as these two visionaries created one of the most beautiful, cutting edge green buildings on the East Coast.

In 2009, the economy tanked, and the bank panicked. Bank of America paralyzed Tim's project. It's true what they say about banks. They don't play fair or nice.

I didn't understand the details of bank foreclosure, (see Tim's chapter for the gory details), but I knew my husband wasn't sleeping at night.

Month after month, Margaret and I kept the Eco-Institute work alive while Tim wrestled with Bank of America.

I didn't care that we were losing $14 million dollars. I cared that Tim sleep again.

After much soul-searching, we sold our house and over 400 acres to pay the bank. We gave away half of our stuff so we could fit into a smaller place.

We asked the Pickards Mountain community to help us move the farm, and people came with shovels, gloves and trucks. We rolled up the fences and dug up the herbs. We caught the chickens and moved the goats to a neighbor's place.

The process felt both frightening and liberating.

I've always been a sucker for frontiers and wilderness: chopping wood, building fires, growing food, pulling together. We hired a couple neighbors and fixed up an old cinderblock cabin on the piece of land we had left.

We camped out in a crumbling old farmhouse for six weeks, amused by the critters we found under the leaky roof with us.

We and the Eco-Instute found a wonderful new home by the pond on our remaining 68 acres. The cabin is sweet and cozy. The farm is thriving. There is food on the table, laughter in our days, and warm beds at night. The PMEI calendar is more full than ever. And Tim is sleeping again.

We still find ourselves in despair sometimes, but we pull each other out of it. We regain our sanity each day by stepping outside, practicing gratitude, putting our hands in the soil, and remembering that life is a sacred opportunity. We know we're living in an incredible moment in time, when the story could take a drastic turn at any moment.

There is a wonderful metaphor I love to share with groups of high schoolers, who are beginning to feel jaded by the magnitude of the crisis and the vast momentum of the current system.

When a caterpillar reaches a certain point in its life, it gets a voracious appetite. It becomes over-consumptive. This triggers the formation of what biologists call "Imaginal Cells." As the caterpillar eats and eats, these imaginal cells begin to vibrate at a different frequency than all the other cells. As the caterpillar makes its cocoon, they begin to find each other.

Then, all the other cells in the caterpillar's body melt into what is called "nutritive soup." They actually UN-differentiate, from being heart cells or brain cells or stem cells, to create this nutritive soup.

The imaginal cells then orchestrate the formation of a completely new being. A butterfly, completely unrecognizable from its earlier state of being.

Our culture is in an over-consumptive state…one which we can't sustain. And amazingly enough, imaginal cells are beginning to appear. We are finding each other and gathering, and have the potential to orchestrate a whole new form of being.

May our understanding continue to evolve, and may we once again find our rightful place in this Sacred Earth Community.

Tim Toben

Tim Toben and I have literally bumped into each other in the small pond that is renewable energy in North Carolina for many years. For awhile there it seemed that every time he was leaving the stage, it was my turn to go on. At symposiums and conferences, and at lectures at local universities, he was the voice of wind energy. And I thought that was odd. Unlike my brother Glen, Tim had never developed a wind project.

All I knew was that he was insanely wealthy, and apparently he had assembled some sort of consortium to develop a wind farm, and in a state that still has zero electricity produced from wind, I figured this must be a good thing. Plus I had heard stories about his hippie wife and their magical mountain.

Whenever I got a chance to listen to Tim—at the legislature, or at a political fund raiser, he always came across as smart, informed and articulate. And whenever we spoke, it was always about venues, and policy, and where the next talk would be.

As my familiarity with Pickards Mountain increased, I started getting to know Tim. One night, in the darkest days of Piedmont, when it appeared as if the bank would be locking the gate, I stood on Tim's front porch while he explained to me the concept of being "all in." He was drunk, and politely saying goodbye to the guests that would occasionally interrupt our conversation. I was also inebriated. And I hung on his every word.

I came off the mountain that night thinking my life could be worse and that I should stop whining, and return to the task at hand: demonstrating a way that humans might sustain life on this garden planet. I believe that's a Thomas Berry phrase. Tim and Megan are Thomas Berry devotees.

What I found most remarkable about Tim was his ability to stay cool under extreme pressure. And to keep his sense of humor in the face of disaster. Tami and I once took my brother Glen up the mountain for dinner, and Tim drilled deep into the logistics of developing a wind project. When we left we were all enlivened by his ability to laugh, and to be joyful in any little thing—from a dinner guest to his wife to fine food on his plate.

After years of us traveling up to Tim and Megan's mountain, one night we invited them to dinner. We live in a ramshackle farmhouse that is best described as a "teardown." Our joke was that their trajectory was coming our way, so we were no longer embarrassed by having them into our home.

We had a delightful night.

Another thing I should say about Tim is that he has been vilified in the local media. As someone who has been through that experience, I understand completely when he just wants to stay home and not go into town until some of the storm has passed.

Finally, I should note that I value Tim for his openness. When I was proposing the solar double-cropping project that was outlined in *Industrial Evolution*, Tim provided me with a copy of his lease arrangement and corporate structure—not to copy directly, but to guide us in how to structure our deal. Clearly his motivation was to see more solar energy come into the world.

At some point I simply became an admirer of Tim's. He's genuine. He gets it. And he is in the fight with everything he has. I feel this is a remarkably candid telling of his story, and I am honored to be presenting it here. As far as I know, it has never been fully told like this...

GREENBRIDGE

Tim Toben

At latest count, there are 300–500 sextillion stars in our universe. That's 300–500 followed by 21 zeros. One of those stars is our sun, and one of the planets that orbit that star is our Earth. Remarkable developments, including the formation of the lithosphere, hydrosphere and atmosphere over the past 4.5 billion years have provided the conditions for the evolution of the myriad forms of life on Earth.

Such is the context for a remarkably insignificant story about eco-activism in the 21st century. For me, it is a story about humility and trust.

My name is Tim Toben. I'm 53 years old, married to woman named Megan, whose smile is as beautiful and gushing as Angel Falls. I have five amazing children—three from a previous marriage and two with Meg. We live on a farm about eight miles west of Carrboro, NC. We have a dairy cow, some horses, two dogs, 30 chickens, two cats, a fish, and an anole that we adopted during a family trip to Sunset Beach.

If you google me, I show up in the business and public policy world of energy and the environment. From that sector,

I've served on academic boards at Duke and UNC-CH, state legislative commissions, and I was appointed the Chairman of the NC Energy Policy Council by our first female governor, the Honorable Beverly Perdue. Recently, I was sipping bourbon on the porch of my friend Scott Crews, when his wife and her friend drove up. Scotty introduced me to Julia's friend as a "Carrlebrity." That's a celebrity in Carrboro (i.e., big fish, little pond). I am the managing partner of Greenbridge Developments, LLC., and that's where this story begins. But first a little background:

I spent my "career" building and running businesses and was pretty good at it. I thought I was really good in 1999, when I sold a business I'd started with $10,000 for $175 million. But in retrospect, I was like most "successful" business people—hard working and DAMNED lucky. My company was Knowledgebase Marketing, Inc. (KBM), a database design and data mining company that served electric utilities, telecommunications companies, and banks.

KBM created relational databases from extracts of client data, cleaned them up, appended publicly available data and performed simple analyses to draw customer profiles for companies. We were an early entry in the "customer relationship management" or CRM space. KBM grew to 350 employees in eight states and three countries. We had an Employee Stock Option Program (ESOP) that generously rewarded our staff when we sold the business. It was a great ride on a capitalist wave that landed us safely on the shores of financial wealth. My share of the sale proceeds was about $10 million.

As its CEO, I worked 12 hour days and traveled three days a week. Although the financial rewards of business were great, the emotional cost was also high. I had a troubled marriage from the outset, but the strains of business augmented our differences and work became a way for me to escape from the unpleasant realities of a failed relationship. I adored my three children, and no one in my family had ever divorced, so I hung on for five years past our 10th anniversary, which was when we essentially began living apart under the same roof.

1999 was also the year that I lost my dad. He was a former Navy pilot—a quiet, disciplined, family man. Both he and my grandfather had been successful textile entrepreneurs. My dad sold his shirt manufacturing business to Wrangler Jeans in Greensboro, and later became its president. His weekends were dedicated to his children and his farm in Guilford County. From the time I was eight until I was 14, even the coldest, wettest Saturdays began with a three-hour walk in the woods with Dad. He never said much, but his love for the tiniest and largest creatures in nature left an indelible imprint on my soul.

In the summer of 1998, dad was diagnosed with non-Hodgkins lymphoma. Dad was 6'1" tall, 180 pounds, and extremely fit for his 68 years. He was a Christian Scientist, and on the rare occasions that he'd been sick prior to that, he'd opted not for medicines, but rather for a trip to the salt water of the ocean, a hard workout, or a rest with a cold rag on his head. Cancer challenged his belief system of "mind over matter." He probably would have chosen against chemotherapy and radiation treatments, but he left that decision to his wife and three sons, who adored him and held out hope that he could be cured.

On January 29, 1999, I laid down next to him in bed. He'd stopped speaking the day before. A precious hospice nurse had been working with us at home for three weeks. The night was grueling. But for the morphine pump, it would have been unbearable. I held his hand through the night, washed his feet and hands with a warm washcloth, as he'd done so many times for me as a child, and watched his respiration drop from 32 to 16 to eight per minute. He died at sunrise on the 30th.

My dad was my best friend, my business mentor, and my original link to nature. The loss I felt was overwhelming—earth-shattering, but something happened that morning that truly surprised me. As I walked my mom upstairs after we said goodbye to dad, the sun rose, a cardinal appeared outside the window, a pair of bluebirds chortled, and then a Carolina wren spoke. Day broke. Honestly, I didn't expect it. Out of the darkness of night and grief, the sun and the graces of nature gave me a glimmer of hope, a taste of life, and the promise of renewal. And so I was, in hindsight, prepared for the death and birth that was to revisit me in another form a decade later.

Greenbridge

After my dad's death, I left my job and retreated into the woods. I sold my stocks and bought 500 acres of rolling hills around Pickards Mountain in western Orange County, NC. My brother Scott and I cut a road in, erected fences for livestock, built a barn, and I placed 143 acres of Chestnut Oak Forest in a "forever wild" conservation easement. In 2000, I began work on a terraced arts and crafts lodge for my family on one of the hillsides overlooking Chapel Hill. It was the ultimate retreat center, albeit way over the top with eight bedrooms and 10 baths. (No matter how many solar panels you slap on a house that size, you're still an energy hog. I clearly had more money than brains.)

In 2002, I met my wife Megan at a Thomas Berry lecture held at the home of my mother, Carolyn. I had dated a few women since my divorce in 1999, but was dubious that I'd ever find a companion with whom to share the balance of my life. It is hard to know when I fell in love with Meg, but it was not long after we met. Meg has written of those times in a separate chapter, so I won't dwell on them, except to add that there has never been a day since April of 2002 that I haven't awakened with profound gratitude for having met her. She is the greatest friend, companion and partner that I could ever imagine. If every person on earth had a partner of such basic goodness and strength of character, there would be no war.

Our relationship is generative. From it, we have birthed two beautiful children, an environmental nonprofit called Pickards Mountain Eco-Institute, and several environmental advocacy initiatives through our affiliations with local schools, universities and state government. In 2005 we were married on our wooded hilltop, surrounded by friends and family, and a pair of red-tailed hawks that circled overhead.

That year, I also purchased most of a city block in downtown Chapel Hill. While serving on the Board of Visitors at Duke University's Nicholas School of the Environment, I'd met the world renowned "green architect" William McDonough. We became friends and in 2004, I traveled with Bill to Iceland on a fishing trip. I had eschewed business for the sake of capitalism, but after a week with Bill and his climate scientist friends, decided that perhaps I could dust off my business skills to advance the cause of reducing carbon emissions through green energy and green building. For that group, reversing the trend in fossil fuel consumption was a moral imperative.

Bill told me that if I'd acquire some urban land for dense infill, he would design a "building like a tree" for our hometown. It would be the building of the future, a national model, a building that produced oxygen, converted sunlight to energy, reused water, and created habitat for hundreds of species with its vegetated roofs.

2005 was the height of the real estate boom, and Chapel Hill was a small town with only one large assemblage of lots remaining in the "town center" zone. It was expensive and owned by the Tate family, whose patriarch had recently died. The property had fallen into severe disrepair over the previous 10 years. The Town of Chapel Hill had designated the block an "economic opportunity zone," in an effort to entice developers to buy it. According to local police, the crime rate on this block was the highest in Chapel Hill. Crack deals and prostitution were commonplace. Yet there was still nostalgia for this block, particularly among the elderly African Americans still living in the area that had fond memories of Nat King Cole and Thelonious Monk playing there 40 or 50 years earlier, at the once-vibrant Starlight Supper Club.

I sold 60 acres of my fairy tale forest to raise the capital to buy 1.25 acres at the corner of Rosemary and Graham Streets. We held a two-day visioning charrette with community organizers, local ministers, public officials, university administrators and investors, facilitated by one of five consulting firms that scored the US Green Building Council's Leadership in Energy and Environmental Design (LEED) buildings. We were intent on a consensus process that was inclusive of all voices in the community and adherent to the highest green building standards. Greenbridge would be a triple bottom-line project, one that balanced the B-Corporation goals of serving people, planet and profit.

Greenbridge was incorporated in January 2006. We agreed on a mission and the principles that would guide our decisions. Five families, including ours, contributed a total of $8.65 million to get the project off the ground. We knew that we would need tens of millions more from a bank to complete Greenbridge, but money was cheap and times were good. Moreover, none of the partners had ever failed in business.

So as Megan took the reins at the farm and built a thriving community-based nonprofit, I became a crusader for green building and eco-social-capitalism. My partners and I embarked on the rather arduous journey of getting a ten-story eco-friendly building permitted in a college town that, despite its progressive claims, was perfectly happy with two-story red brick. A breakthrough came in October of 2006, when our popular and outspoken State Senator Ellie Kinnaird wrote the following letter to the Chapel Hill newspaper:

I understand there is concern over the changing streetscape of Chapel Hill as proposed by Greenbridge. As a newcomer in 1964, I was amazed to see the unified colonial style of commercial buildings. I was amused to see colonial gas stations, bus stations, and grocery stores in the 20th century. Eventually the style became the semi-official vocabulary of the town.

But just as historic is the expression of each generation's aspirations reflected in their architecture. We are fortunate to have an expression today that reflects our great love for and stewardship of our environment. Our goal of preservation now is our planet's preservation. What could better epitomize this than a completely green building, and one of magnificent architectural design?

Even if one were concerned over mimicking late 20th century architectural design, Rosemary Street has never had distinctive buildings. Greenbridge is a rare opportunity to show the world we are serious about our leadership in carbon reduction through building and living our ideals.

Meanwhile, my partners and I were operating on several fronts. Michael Cucchiara led the design team and worked closely with McDonough and his team in Charlottesville, VA. He engaged a local architect, Josh Gurlitz, to take the design development (concept) drawings to construction (blueprint) drawings. Tom Tucker was responsible for community relations. Beyond the 15 public hearings that were required by the Town Council and its planners over the two year process, we voluntarily held local meetings at the neighborhood community center to make sure that the entire community, even those who declined to attend public hearings, was aware of what was happening. Tom and I even walked door to door and surveyed residents to make certain that everyone was informed and able to provide input.

I was responsible for legal, finance and PR. In early 2008, Greenbridge received unanimous approval from the Chapel Hill Town Council. We were complimented for our innovation and for our inclusive plan dedicated to people and planet, and not just profit. Our design was named one of the ten most sustainable projects in America by *Natural Home* magazine.

We broke ground on April 2, 2008, and began excavating a 30-foot hole over the entire 1.25 acres of land. Our agreement with Bank of America was that they would loan us the $43.5 million needed to complete the project, provided we spent our $8.65 million in equity first. They also required every partner to "jointly and severally guarantee" the construction loan.

What that means in layman's terms is that if, for any reason, the project fails, each partner is personally responsible for repaying the entire balance of the loan. Those words are standard language in loans of this nature and magnitude. Nonetheless, they did give us, and our legal council, considerable pause. But we were successful entrepreneurs, the top-gun pilots of the business world. And none of us had been shot at, much less shot down.

It was June 2008. The banks were sensing a storm on the horizon and beginning to behave strangely. We were three months into our excavation, three weeks away from our loan closing, and beyond the point of no return, when BofA sent us a letter with "a few new terms" to our loan. These conditions were non-negotiable. They had us over a barrel. Among the terms, (1) they asked us to hire a development manager (not us) that was "bank approved," and (2) they wanted us to contribute another $5 million of equity, before they would approve the loan. So in an instant, we were fired from our own project and replaced with their confederates, and we had to raise $5 million in three weeks.

Needless to say, we were stunned. We could stop the project and walk away from our $8.65 million in design, permitting, and excavation costs over the past 30 months, or we could agree to those terms. It was too late to find another bank, and only Wachovia, BofA, and Citibank were doing deals above $25 million without syndication (partners).

Navy pilots never say die and we believed in our mission, so we called everyone we knew. Through our acquaintance with Senator John Edwards, Michael and I had met a gentleman named Fred Baron, who was a famed defense attorney, having earned his fortune suing asbestos manufacturers. Fred agreed to fly out from Texas to have lunch with us. His wife Lisa was intrigued by the possibility of investing in a national model for green building. At the end of our 45 minute lunch at 411 West on Franklin Street, Fred offered to loan us $3 million, provided his loan was to us personally, and not to Greenbridge. The annual interest rate would be 18%, but we saw it as short-term debt that could be replaced with institutional debt, once the bank loan was secured. Like the bank debt, this "mezzanine" financing would be personally guaranteed. We accepted his offer and were 60% closer to our goal. With the $3 million committed, partners, spouses, and friends anted up and made up the balance. With a figurative gun to our heads, we signed the bank documents and accepted their "development manager." The die was cast.

In October 2008, we were days away from closing on replacement financing for our mezzanine debt (Baron, friends and family), when the stock market crashed. The Wall Street banks, ours included, had gambled and lost, and the US economy headed into a tailspin. Hardest hit were the real estate and housing markets, and Greenbridge was at that intersection. Our institutional lender withdrew his offer to refinance the mezz debt. We still had nine months before the notes were due, so we didn't panic. We'd pre-sold over half of all units, so we remained confident that we could weather the storm and that the market would recover.

What kept us going at each of these challenging junctures was the belief that what we were doing was fundamentally "good." Of the three legs of the triple bottom-line stool, our shortest was profit. Surely, the Universe or God wouldn't let this project fail. It was too important for society (people) and the environment (planet).

Two 150' cranes went up and the project began rising out of the ground. A professor at UNC Chapel Hill who had a penchant for writing about gentrification seized on Greenbridge as a target. A small group of white students from her class began meeting with residents of the historically African American neighborhood adjacent to Greenbridge. Posters began appearing on telephone poles around town reading "Greenbridge is Racist," and "Stop Gentrification." This formidable structure rising out of the ground was an easy target, even as studies showed that five years before Greenbridge was launched, 70% of the neighborhood was owned by developers, who were renting homes to mostly white university students. Indeed, gentrification had quietly crept in over the previous 30 years.

Although we'd endured numerous, and sometimes colossal, headaches with Greenbridge, this was the first heartache. One of our partners, Frank Phoenix, was the leading philanthropist in the community for the local chapter of Habitat for Humanity. Our office was in the African American neighborhood and many of the elders of that community were close friends and strong supporters. I often shared lunch with the matriarchs of the community, listening to their wisdom and receiving their blessings. Meg sent them greens and tomatoes from the garden, and one of them called me an "angel sent to revitalize their community, an answer to her prayers." Despite their attempts to dispel this notion, the newspapers picked up on the story and soon a few recruits from the local anarchist community joined the chorus. The project was vandalized and twice was the target of bomb threats, halting construction while bomb sniffing dogs scoured the construction site.

By the fall of 2009, things were getting silly. We were halfway finished and pre-sales were limping along. The bank was behaving oddly again. Banks, after all, are staffed by people, and bank managers tend to be some of the least creative thinkers in the business world. With fallout from their own risky behavior raining down on them, they were being asked to refinance and extend loans, while regulators were tightening down on their lending practices. No one was lending a dime to developers.

Costs crept higher as the prototype building began incorporating its green technologies. It was clear that we were going to need another $2 million on top of the $59.5 million already budgeted, and there was only one place to look for new capital—ourselves. We dug deep and liquidated assets. I was now "all-in" with my liquid assets in Greenbridge, and my house and land were pledged to the bank and to mezzanine creditors, who had extended their loans for another year. The partners and mezzanine debts were now up to $18 million on top of the bank's $43.5 million.

We all held our breath as we approached the finish line in June 2010. The project was spectacular in form and function. Contract holders began to close on their units. In just the first 90 days, we closed on 37 of the 97 residences. It looked like we might actually survive this ordeal and deliver on our dream green building, against all odds.

Then the contractor delivered a final bill. We would

be $1.6 million short. Our pockets were empty. There was only one place to go to cover the final 1.5% of costs...Bank of America. Surely, they would see the wisdom in finishing the project and continuing the sales momentum that we had built. After a month's long wait for their answer, they proved true to form and declined. The contractor stopped work and placed construction liens on the project. Without clean title to the property, we couldn't close the remaining units under contract. Sales were halted. We had to turn away families who wanted to buy homes in Greenbridge. Without sales, we had no way to service the debt. It was over. We were in default and facing a $30 million call on the bank note and $9 million in calls from mezz creditors. Greenbridge would be taken over by the bank, and we would all lose everything we owned.

It's one thing to lose all you have, if you're the only person affected. It's quite another to lose your family home and the property on which your wife operates a thriving nonprofit. I had a friend who went through the same crash as a real estate developer in South Carolina. His response was to put a bullet in his head. I cannot know how desperate he was, nor judge his suicide, but I have visited the abyss, and it is terrifying.

Fortunately, I had Meg, the kids, and a sense of humor. How naive it was for me to think that we would somehow be spared, and treated differently by a bank, because of our social and ecological values. Their corporate PR said they cared about that stuff, but their loan officers hadn't gotten the memo. We were just another building project with cost overruns and the bank wasn't lending. As our banker said, "it's nothing personal." So why do they call themselves "personal bankers?" It is the entrepreneurs that take the risks and create the jobs, and so I did feel resentful that it was the bank's risky bets on Wall Street that led to the conditions that crushed the little guys on main street.

Meg never missed a beat. "I love you Tim Toben. We'll just move down to the pond and live in the old lake house. We can move the nonprofit down there too," she said. We still had one lovely parcel that was protected from creditors, by virtue of the fact that it was co-owned by us both in a legal structure called "tenants by the entirety." Since she hadn't signed the loans, creditors could not collect on her assets, so we began packing up. Everything I owned had to be liquidated—home, land, cash—to pay off the debt.

It took us eight months. The lake house is over 100 years old. It has no heat, the floors are falling in from decades of termite infestations, the paint on the walls was lead-based. Not the ideal domicile in which to raise small children. Twice at night, I got up to use the bathroom and stepped on frogs. We chose to renovate an adjacent cinder block building, but had only the money that we'd borrowed from my mom and brother. So we rolled up our sleeves, recruited a few friends and neighbors, and within four months created our casita by the pond.

Megan put out a request for help to the community that supported Pickards Mountain Eco-Institute. During the same four month period, over 100 volunteers moved fences, farm equipment, camp shelters and even soil that we'd enriched with years of leaf mulch and compost. I did vigorous physical labor on the house or land for at least five hours a day, which, along with walks in the woods, kept me sane as I navigated the numerous legal land mines with the bank and creditors.

I revisited a few influential authors, who had given me insight and inspiration after my father's death—Thomas Berry, E. F. Schumacher, Alfred North Whitehead. Their message was that change is inevitable and precious. The universe itself is precarious, and we must live our lives fully and in the service of future generations. Greenbridge began to shrink as a mental construct. The geese landing on the pond, the sound of my two-year-old laughing, and long walks and conversations with family and friends filled the void. Meg's love and loyalty were constant.

I received a call from Governor Perdue some months after the Greenbridge meltdown. She believed in what we had attempted and had appointed me Chairman of the NC Energy Policy Council to help promote a low-carbon energy future for the state. Her first words to me were "Screw Bank of America." I laughed. Then she said "Tim, you'll pick yourself up and be right back where you were financially in no time." Her comments were well intentioned but they rang hollow. "No Bev, I've ridden the roller coaster of capitalism, and it's time to get off." I thanked her for her call.

Beyond fatigue, my readings and experience also led me to the conclusion that green capitalism was not a solution to the ecological and social crises facing the world. Our form of capitalism was, in fact, the central problem. In an op-ed to the Durham *Herald*, I wrote:

> It turns out that no matter how many of us trade our SUVs for hybrids or move to homes within biking or walking distance from work and schools, we're still doomed by consumerism and our national appetite for GDP growth. The big picture has become clear— as GDP grows, restorative ecosystems shrink. The

bipartisan mantra is jobs, jobs, jobs, but how does economic growth serve future generations?

On the current economic roadmap, all growth is good. An industry that pollutes the air, water, or soil or extracts minerals from an indigenous community is as prized as a non-polluting industry that builds community or restores ecosystems. Both produce material throughput, jobs, profits and taxes.

But is this indiscriminate model sustainable? (If all growth was good, we gardeners wouldn't have to weed…) Sustainability was defined by the United Nations as "the ability of the current generation to meet its needs without compromising the ability of future generations to meet theirs."

The financial system upon which the global economy is based fails to monitor and adapt to limits imposed by (1) finite natural resources, (2) the carrying capacity of ecosystems, and (3) the growing wealth disparity between nations and between the rich and the poor within nations. Global trade imbalances, centralized monetary systems, structural fiscal imbalances and crumbling infrastructure increase the risk of ruptures like the one experienced in October 2008.

Most threatening of all, the material throughput of the economic system is breaching the boundaries of the biosphere. A condition known as "ecological overshoot" exists, whereby the global economy is now using up more than 1.4 times the earth's capacity to regenerate the natural capital upon which the system and all life depends. This unintended consequence derives from the assumption that the resources and regenerative capacities of the earth are limitless, which, of course, is false.

More troubling than the four-fold increase in the human population during the 20th century was a 40-fold increase in GDP, accompanied by a 16-fold increase in fossil fuel use, a 35-fold increase in fisheries catches, a 30 percent loss of arable soil in the past 40 years, the draining of underground aquifers, the melting of glaciers, the accumulation of atmospheric CO_2, the degradation and warming of the oceans, and toxic chemical accumulation globally. We are shredding the fabric of life upon which the economy depends and, more critically, on which *all life* depends.

So where do we go from here? I concur with economists at the new economics foundation in London. A "no growth" or negative growth model is our only hope for the seventh generation ahead. One author whose work I admire is Derrick Jensen, who takes it a step further and advocates for dismantling the industrial growth economy by forming a robust resistance movement. The Occupy Movement is one piece of such a model, which specifically assails the concentration of wealth among the top 1% at the expense of society and the environment. I wholeheartedly support that effort.

After reading Jensen's *Deep Green Resistance*, I attended several book readings at the Internationalist Book Store in Chapel Hill. There, I met some of the "anarchists" who'd protested Greenbridge. I wanted to understand their objections better and place them in the context of eco-activism. Finally, it was clear to me. To them, Greenbridge was a threat to the movement opposing an industrial model. It served to delude the mainstream into believing that we could solve these global crises by "greening" America and the world. Unfortunately, all credible science suggests that we must depart from the current economic model, very fast, abandon capitalism, and rebuild resilient local economies that can sustain the shocks that lie ahead.

So Meg and I are growing fruit and nut trees, berry bushes and vegetables by the pond. We're raising catfish and butchering deer given to us by neighbors who hunt. Our farm runs on solar power and our life is much simpler. We take walks as a family and invite friends for long conversations. We're in our second year of hosting the Carrboro-Chapel Hill Storytellers Group on Monday nights, and we're trying to imagine and create a future without fossil fuels or globalization. We invite everyone who's interested to visit us, attend workshops and potlucks, and if moved to do so, make donations to support the work of the nonprofit. Time will tell whether this model is sustainable, but I'm sleeping again, caring for my land and family, and life has never been better.

If someone had told me a year ago, when I was facing a $39 million debt, that in one year I would be happier and more fulfilled than ever before in my life, I'd have scoffed. Indeed, the Universe/God did provide, in a mysterious way, the future that I'd always dreamed of, and my trust in this ecstatic universe has never been greater. It also turns out that a little humility goes a long way towards making life a whole lot more fun and real.

So once again, out of the darkness of night and grief, the sun and the graces of nature have given me a glimmer of hope, a taste of life, and the promise of renewal.

Rebekah Hren

I first met Rebekah when she was dipping her toe in the water of the solar installation industry. She was thinking about doing it for a living, and sure enough, she went on to become an installer, and an educator, and a writer of wonderful "how to" books. Her first was the *The Carbon Free Home*, which was packed with do-it-yourself projects based on her retrofit of an old house in Durham, North Carolina. She then came out with the *Solar Buyers Guide*, which helped readers navigate the maze that is the solar equipment industry.

Rebekah has led workshops for the Abundance Foundation, and teaches for Solar Energy International out in Colorado. During my nights at the kitchen table with Rebekah I have found her to be curious, and searching, and incredibly alive.

She and her first husband, Stephen once built a phenomenal house out of cob. And they once held a potluck in which all of the food was to be foraged from Dumpsters, or harvested by the old Roman law of usufruct, or acquired in some other "free" way.

I was stressed about what to take to such an event. Not being a Dumpster diver, I was worried I might not have a "cool" enough offering to take to the party. That day I was catching up on some work at the biodiesel plant, and when I headed back into town I noticed a dead squirrel in the road. Since it had not been there upon my arrival, I figured it had been freshly killed. So I stopped. And it was still warm. No flies. No ants. Fresh.

I took it back to the plant kitchen, cleaned it, dressed it, and boiled it for awhile to make it tender. Squirrels are tough right off the tree. When I arrived at Rebekah's party, my offering was roadkill squirrel, and with that I fit in fine.

Rebekah has been thinking deeply about renewable energy for years. She's made her own fuel, she's run around on straight vegetable oil, and perhaps more importantly, she has worked hard on ways to dispense fuel with the help of active and passive solar strategies.

After many years in the movement, here is her take.

MORE QUESTIONS
THAN ANSWERS

Rebekah Hren

If you are thumbing through the pages looking for the literary equivalent to, say, Shostakovich's Symphony #10, Movement 2—an invigorating chapter that will make you feel
like throwing open a window and shouting out, "watch out
world, here comes change!", I'm sorry to tell you that this will
not be it. This chapter leans more towards a crisis of faith,
towards doubters in need of companionship, towards the
weary and wondering. (And besides, I wouldn't want you to
throw open a window if it were cold out and you've got the
fireplace humming.)

Here's my story.

At 15 I started to doubt the world. At 20 I gazed with a
mix of excitement and trepidation at my very own 10 acres
tucked in the woods, full of possibilities, debating the rela-
tive merits of underground houses, strawbale, monolithic
concrete, nomadic Mongolian dwelling, kerosene lamps and
pit toilets. I spent my days learning to plumb and reading

about self-sufficiency. At 27 I graduated to scraping lead paint from endless yards of salvaged wood in fits and starts of house restoration projects, learning to wire solar panels, proselytizing about peak oil. At 30 I moved on to writing DIY sustainability books and hooking up illegal greywater tanks in the city. Edging closer to 40 now, I wonder why: why I feel so damn guilty leaving the refrigerator open one second longer than absolutely necessary (or having a refrigerator at all); why I long for a thermostat on the wall; why I save nearly every piece of plastic that crosses my path, why I can't in good conscience buy strawberries in January.

Don't get me wrong, these words are not a lament or regret for paths chosen; rather, it's a desire to understand. I didn't start out on this path because of peak oil or climate change or industrial food, but because of an unsettling certainty that something wasn't quite right with the way the world goes about its business. The more I learned, the more this feeling was confirmed. As the years went by, the choice became stark: retreat inwards, wall myself off, and live with the growing despair that comes with feeling ineffectual and powerless, or direct my actions and gaze outwards and try to become an agent of change—and look for respite in the trying.

Nearly a decade ago I received a birthday card from close relatives with a lovely photo of a nature scene on the front, and the hand-printed message inside "…there is still beauty in the world." Well, that certainly gave me pause, wondering exactly what was meant by that cryptic message. Was I wrong to interpret the statement as a perspective on how my relatives viewed me: Debbie-downer, thinking the world was so grey and gloomy that I needed reminding it wasn't all bad? Was I really the person portrayed by this one-line sentiment? I reacted with mixed emotions—reflection, anger, bewilderment and curiosity. I've thought back on that card many times over the following years, reflecting on how my attitude has changed over time.

My role as agent of change started off a little rocky, and yes I spent some time spewing gloom and doom. Peak oil, climate change, air, water and food pollution, GMO crops, oil spills, lack of community, the charade of democracy, yeah, the list goes on and I've gone through the stages of grief. I've built the proverbial off-grid bunker, stockpiled food, grown my own fowl. Decided the hell with it, if the shit hits the fan, I'd rather go out in a quick flame than a slow starvation. Moved to the gritty middle of a city to attempt to be an island of information per Richard Heinberg's wise instructions. Tried in vain to scrub every last ounce of fossil fuels from my life. (By the way, the constant ministrations needed by an 80-year-old house, running off renewable energy, surrounded by an edible urban landscape, are astonishing.)

I learned a lot.

I learned that taking action in the face of seemingly insurmountable problems makes you feel great. Taking action can build stronger communities and networks, even if it doesn't move you much closer towards solutions to problems of global scale. And strong communities are rare, sweet, and still all-too-easily dissoluble.

I learned that the more rules you make for yourself and those around you, the more rules there are to be made. I learned that I'm not good at telling people what to do.

I've gone through periodic episodes of living a relatively public life: book tours; speaking engagements; radio, magazine, newspaper and video interviews; even near-monthly public tours of my house complete with labels explaining the recycled eco-friendly clean-energy solutions on display. Talked with or been heard by thousands of people across the country. So of course I've often been asked how I became an "environmentalist." Was it my parents' influence, or maybe a schoolteacher, or perhaps a book I read? I honestly I don't know the answer, and the question confuses me. As far back as I can remember it was perfectly clear to me that we only have one earth, and we should be trying our damndest to keep it in good shape if we want to continue living here. Combined with even a tiny speck of empathy for other people and species, I don't know how you couldn't "become" an "environmentalist."

I go back to that birthday card—if I didn't perceive the beauty left in the world, would I not be an entirely different sort of person? Perhaps one who doesn't make friends and family feel like they have to lie about how often they use their dryer? Being an environmentalist isn't nearly as simple as it sounds, and the word itself does not nearly cover the breadth of awareness necessary to comprehend the network of issues facing and endangering us. We are way past those save-the-whales days. Every road keeps forking, the decision tree branches and those darn butterflies keep flapping away somewhere across the deep blue sea. Do my actions make a difference? If not, why do I try? If so, then how can I morally keep using Styrofoam and flying by jet plane?

The rules of engagement are incredibly messy. If my actions matter, then shouldn't one of my actions be to continue proselytizing to the masses about why the way they live is damaging, harmful, and irresponsible? Occasionally when I visit ~~my parents~~ (name blacked out to protect the innocent), they hide the Folger's in the cupboard and put the fair-trade shade-grown organic coffee out on the counter. After enduring dozens of my logical, rational, utterly convincing talks on home energy efficiency, they still won't add storm windows to their 80-year-old single-pane windows. I must admit they did submit to installing a barely functional solar air heater that looks much like a UFO on their urban roof, although I secretly think it was the tax credit argument they succumbed to more than the clean energy argument. The sad thing is, after years of pondering, I honestly don't know what actions are valid responses to the current crises (but I do know you should get storm windows, Mom and Dad).

So what to do? This isn't a game—I believe the world as we know it is at stake. Every action necessitates consideration. Perhaps I should wear only clothes made of organic cotton. Maybe local-made clothes are better than organic cotton clothes—or second-hand clothes, you know, like recycling—but wait, is recycling ok? Maybe it's better to stop buying glass and metal containers altogether, and only purchase what can be bought in bulk. Walk everywhere. Eat only local vegetables. Live in a cave with no heat. Cook over an open fire. Or better yet: cave-dwelling raw food nudist drinking only spring water and bathing in the rain.

OK, that's obviously crazy talk. How about I try, at the very least, to balance each selfish oblivious earth and community destroying act with an equal act of nurture and mindfulness? But I was never that good at math. Perhaps the answer is to find one undoubtedly useful thing I'm good at and focus on that, and ignore the rest of the calculations. Choose a right-livelihood, and reap some personal benefits by not having to worry so much about the rest of the mess we're in. Pretend like there is an invisible scale where the good I do can outweigh the bad.

I've got a fairly right-livelihood, as these things go. I'm a solar electrician, system designer and educator. At first I wanted to install only off-grid battery-based solar electric systems. Screw the utility and their base rates and nox and sox emissions, let the grid fail, we can make our electricity. A few years later I was convinced (with prodding from some intelligent friends) that the utility grid was actually a blessing in disguise, and started installing grid-tied systems, to help support the grid and reverse eminent domain. As if in the blink of an eye, now I'm helping build 20+ acre solar farms. Can one tiny solar system help our current host of problems? How about five medium-sized? Ten gigantic ones? How about teaching other people how to build systems—you know that proverb about teaching a man to fish.

Honestly I don't much care what the answer is, because I love my job. I'm lucky it's a job that fits my definitions of helpful rather than harmful (though I chose it for that reason so it wasn't actually luck). It is also a technical job, studying the National Electrical Code and wire sizing calculations mean I can often forget about academic questions such as whether corn-based ethanol makes the price of tortillas rise in Mexico and adds strain to the lives of millions.

I've talked to hundreds of people around the country who want to be in my shoes, with a meaningful, engaging occupation rather than a job of soul-wrenching tedium, or no job at all. The question I frequently get is "how?" How can I move from this space to that other place, the one where I feel right about my actions? How can I balance three kids and a mortgage with the desire for a right livelihood? How 'bout you shouldn't have had that third kid in the first place buddy! But who am I to judge? And therein lies the problem.

I don't know if it matters that you live in a 10,000 square foot house with two hummers, six kids, and an Olympic-sized heated pool. Maybe you donate 50% of your income to promote clean drinking water in developing countries, and I should just shut the hell up about the excess of kilowatt-hours you burn through keeping your pool warm. I'm often tempted to answer the "what can I do?" question with "every little bit helps"—hey, turn down your pool heater a notch, run the hummer off biodiesel. But that's utter bullshit, ya know? We are in a deep morass of trouble here, and little bits here and there just aren't going to suffice.

It comes back time and again to that old theme, from countless books and narratives. Would you rather open your eyes, recognize the crumbling lattice of society's unhealthy and unstable structure surrounding you, and find yourself forever-after struggling like Sisyphus with that blasted rock? Or would you rather drink the kool-aid of mass culture, and enjoy it while it lasts?

Because I think about all the incredible problems in the world and just wilt. The fact that rural women in India drop out of school as soon as they begin menstruation because they can't afford sanitary napkins. Hospitals in Haiti with no electricity at all, rhinos killed for only their horn, indigenous languages going extinct, the Pacific Garbage Patch, the few small glaciers left at Glacier National Park disappearing within twenty years, and on and on. Sure, you can choose your battles, but the war rages on.

And there is still beauty left in the world, for now.

I believe I've regressed to a more private life for the time being. I'm not currently that interested in being a role model, or a person people turn to with their earnest and searching questions, in a world where I honestly don't know what to do, nor do I know what to tell you to do.

Bigger picture—I say forget about it. Throw out your TV, ride a bike, grow your own food, turn your thermostat down, stop eating meat. Sounds good to me, if you can put on blinders and ignore the other 8 billion people on the planet sunning themselves on the decks of the *Titanic*. I might be bitter, or maybe just burned out. I won't be the first and certainly not the last to be humbled by the scope and scale of the issues, and by the wanton disregard shown by many of those around me.

So I'm going to lie here on the beach and daydream, go whale-watching, enjoy the moment, think about the beauty still left in the world.

Blair L. Pollock

I hardly know Blair at all, aside from hearing him speak and reading his columns in the Chapel Hill *News*. But I have always known him as the guy who brought recycling to Chapel Hill and Orange County. To me he has always been in a bureaucratic role, and he has always been different.

Ten years ago, when I was teaching a renewable energy class at Central Carolina Community College, in the very early days of biodiesel, Blair was the only public official I knew who was talking about climate change. He was blunt about it. At that time George W. Bush was in power, and the term "global warming" was not allowed at any Department of Energy sponsored conferences.

One time I was working with the Orange Water and Sewer Authority (OWASA) on fueling their fleet, and I was surprised to see them flaring the methane at their waste-water facility. OWASA is famous for its progressive approach to waste water treatment, and they lead the region with "best practices."

I commented on it to Blair and he replied, "That's nothing. We are not even flaring at the landfill. The emissions coming off that landfill alone offset all of the recycling we have done to date."

For some reason that discarded comment hit me like a sledgehammer. Blair was responsible for recycling, and he was putting all of his hard work into context with a single remark. I was stunned.

And inspired. I figured that if a government official could be open and honest about the work that lies before us, there was hope.

Here is Blair's story....

DOING NEW THINGS

Blair L. Pollock

It's hard to reckon when my journey to becoming a tree-hugger began. Some environmental psychologists say that those who spend more time in the woods or outdoors in general between ages six and eleven are much more likely to be imbued with a love of nature. I did and I am.

At sixty, I've now spent the past 25 years developing, operating and planning recycling and waste reduction programs for Orange County, North Carolina. For ten years before that in both Chapel Hill and Memphis, I was involved in energy conservation and renewable energy work. Pairing the personal with the professional, I spent time on some local boards, helping initiate the Town of Chapel Hill's Bicycle and Pedestrian Advisory Board and serving for 18 years on a homeowners' board that focused mostly on protecting water quality in Lake Ellen, the little urban water body at the heart of my former neighborhood.

At every chance, I've hiked the local woods, measured water quality in "my" lake, and been hands-on in my passion. I still don't hesitate to literally get my (gloved) hands dirty doing the occasional waste composition study. I also recognize the power of the media in advancing the cause. I write about environmental issues for professional publications and local general media, including a two year stint for *The Menorah*, a local monthly Jewish journal, taking a theological perspective on environmental matters.

I am featured monthly on a local radio station to talk about solid waste and have collaborated on scripts and production for a few public television environmental documentaries. Over the past 15 years I've been interviewed for a couple of solid waste documentaries for WUNC public television and on public access TV as well. Occasionally I engage in state or national political discourse, usually via the internet. I have mostly kept a local focus, believing in that adage, "think globally, act locally."

Neither of my parents was particularly nature-oriented. We didn't go camping, birdwatching or anything like that. Golf, ballgames or trips to the beach were more likely family outdoor pursuits. But probably more importantly, my folks didn't stop my brother and me from going into the "woods" behind our house or down the street (and by "woods," I mean a small strip of suburban oak buffer between our backyard and the Southern State Parkway in Seaford on Long Island). The strip of woods extended maybe a quarter-mile, half the length of Alken Avenue in an early suburb on the island, and aside from some pretty bad teachers, about all I remember from age five to eight is playing in those woods with my brother and my friends.

My best friend Billy and I caught a garter snake one day before school. Billy had learned, I'm not sure how, to safely hold the snake right behind the head squeezing lightly with thumb and forefinger and he showed me this trick. We took turns carrying him, angry and squirming, from the woods and put him (maybe it was a her?) in a cardboard box we'd carefully weighted down with rocks. We were sure we had a new pet, but when we got home from school, he'd escaped.

Billy also knew about sassafras and taught me how to distinguish it from all other plants by its unique pattern of three differently shaped leaves on the same plant. We were fascinated by the root beer smell of the plant's roots, and were determined to make our own root beer. Pulling up massive amounts of the roots and bringing them into my parents' basement, we washed them off and pounded them on the concrete floor with the hammers from my dad's work bench to release the flavor. Then we were going to soak the roots in seltzer, add sugar and we'd have our root beer. Of course my mother heard the industrious pounding, interrupted and quickly put a stop to that nonsense, assuring us we'd poison ourselves with those roots anyway. So began my fascination with the natural world.

In six subsequent summers I spent a month at sleep-away camp, where I learned to canoe, ride horses, camp and got to spend more unstructured time in the woods. The first couple of years, my brother and I tried to bring home some of the bright orange, spotted salamanders that filled the Pocono Mountains woods after each heavy rain. Shortly before camp ended we'd get big steel cans from the camp kitchen, fill them with moss and soil, put a few salamanders in each and carry them on the bus home. Despite our efforts to keep the soil moist, within a few days of arriving home, we could find no evidence of life, not even a skeleton. I wonder now if those same woods are still populated with so many salamanders that you could find them under each bit of moss. Given the worldwide amphibian decline, I fear not.

Fifty years later, I see I've had a career in environmental activism of various kinds and feel good about most of it. The whole path was not intentional but the passion was, and there is no other place where I found a fit. Now it's kind of bittersweet when some old friends introduce me as the "Recycling Czar of Chapel Hill" and I believe I once was. Now, instead, I am a kind of slightly fossilized bureaucrat with a decent salary, health plan, benefits and a view towards some kind of retirement on the horizon. But my idea of retirement (and don't tell my wife), is a two-year state-wide walk from county seat to county seat across North Carolina, picking up roadside can and bottle litter that wouldn't be there if there were a bottle bill. I envision dumping my collection of discarded cans and bottles on the steps of each County courthouse to great fanfare (due to my constant blogging) as I stump for North Carolina to be the first Southern state to pass a bottle bill.

Even in a comfortable office, I get fired up daily about some aspect of the outrage that's inflicted on our planet and try to act, even if it's a mouse click, a phone call or a newspaper article. To survive the grim daily onslaught of negative information, I also try to maintain a sense of humor, spontaneity, creativity and trust in my non-environmentally obsessed fellows to care at least somewhat about the issues too. I still pluck a can or bottle a day off the street to recycle as my antidote to despair. They're always there when you look down.

So what exactly is this environmental career and when did it begin? The part where I began to make a living from working in my chosen field was upon leaving graduate school at age 27. Before that there was a bit of communing with nature while I traveled, some wilderness camping, lots of swimming in lakes, ponds and oceans, and some dilettantish college activism (including the thwarted "guerrilla theater" attempt to pour motor oil all over a Texaco recruiter's desk)...and a lot of early recycling. There was also a lame and poorly executed undergraduate photography project documenting the first Earth Day and local pollution around Madison, Wisconsin in April 1970. I got a well deserved D, never quite having mastered the technical skills of the darkroom, let alone properly matting a picture.

The anti-war activism of that time also infused and informed my attitude towards making environmental change, and I soon realized that the change was going to have to be on multiple fronts, and there was no one way to stop the war on the planet. I still continue to realize that multiple approaches—from the direct action of Greenpeace-type protests to growing large scale community gardens through the excruciating process of passing and enforcing new environmental laws—have to all be part of the mix, and I vary my own approaches too.

My ADHD has probably served me well over the course of my career, as has my lack of interest in making financial prosperity my highest priority. It's not like I'm an ascetic or don't appreciate material goods, it has just never been the most important thing.

Professionally, I've never held a job that someone else had before me or held after me. I created all three environmental jobs I've held over the past thirty-three years, and was hired by people who generally were also starting out down the same path with as little or less inkling than I what they wanted from the positions they'd created or hired me for. Fortunately for me, I was a fit for their organizations and each of those three times I found in retrospect, I was the only interviewee.

Perhaps it's useful to wander down the career path a bit. When I came to Chapel Hill to graduate school in City and Regional Planning in the fall of 1976, I held a BA from the University of Wisconsin in a self-styled independent major that I'd grandiosely termed "Urban Planning and Environmental Studies."

Due to my early urban planning reading, I ended up spending the summer of 1972 at Paolo Soleri's Arcosanti, the prototype of his arcologies (Soleri's made-up word for his idealized ecological architecture). This futuristic vision was and is still being erected in the desert outside Scottsdale, Arizona and at this time of writing, Paolo is 92 and still at it. That summer, I lived in an eight-by-eight concrete cube with four-foot diameter open circles in each wall and the ceiling. I worked from five in the morning until two in the blazing afternoon, building what was literally supposed to become that shining city on the hill. Utopians from all over the country paid to work this hard in 100-degree heat, in exchange for three meals a day and the altruistic visionary notion that we were forging a new way. When I Google some of my fellows, I see that many are still deeply involved in environmental/ urban pursuits. So something about that time and place and spirit resonated through the forty intervening years. Some of the same spirit still infuses me.

That was the early 1970s. The EPA had just been formed, the first Federal Clean Air and Clean Water act were just being formulated, the Santa Barbara oil spill had just polluted the pristine southern California coast, and the Arab Oil embargo of 1973–4 gave us the first real glimpse of the geopolitics of energy. The first ripples of Rachel Carson and Aldo Leopold's seminal work were being concretized for the public as their acolytes went forth as policymakers, activists, elected officials and teachers.

By the time I hit graduate school in 1976, it was halcyon days for environmental activism: Jimmy Carter became president and put solar panels on the White House, and Federal money became available for everything from local energy conservation plans to multimillion dollar wastewater plant upgrades so that rivers would no longer catch fire.

The first and second oil embargoes added considerable lift to the early energy conservation and solar movement. The Solar Lobby started up in 1978. Shortly afterwards, I helped erect the first attached solar greenhouse in Chapel Hill on the Pine Knolls community center. The vision was for kids from this poor black neighborhood to use the greenhouse to grow seedlings they could sell, while the excess heat would warm the adjoining center, lowering heating bills.

While in graduate school, I'd started to work part time for a start-up energy conservation consulting firm, Integrated Energy Systems. The company owner gave me not only a job but a slot on the Alternative Energy Task Force for then first-time gubernatorial candidate Jim Hunt. Before he hired me, I told my new boss Dan Koenigshofer that I knew no engineering, couldn't work a scientific calculator, and I knew nothing about North Carolina politics. Dan put me right to work, all the way through graduate school and beyond. While in the classroom I took one course in solar design and one in which I created an inventory of the potential for "biomass for energy in North Carolina, tearing into the agricultural census and extrapolating animal manure availability from the number of confined hogs and chickens and dairy cattle statewide. A short thirty-five years later, methane from manure is catching on, thanks to tax credits and global climate change. Energy prices don't have that much to do with it.

In that all-important summer between graduate school years, I could have gone to DC and been an intern for the then very new Council on Environmental Quality that Carter had started, or I could have stayed outside doing another field summer. I chose the front range of Colorado at Elizabeth Wright-Ingraham Institute over smog laden DC. Another summer outdoors in a tent with no running water and hard field work every day for no money—such a deal. At least I had a scholarship this time. Instead of gravitating towards being a bureaucrat-in-training, which would have been the right career move for sure, I went into the fields—a heart-move for sure.

Shortly after the end of graduate school, the great burst of energy consulting work began to peter out for our firm, energy prices had calmed down. After a very slim winter, I suddenly found myself with three job interviews, one in Memphis, running a very hands-on job training program in solar and energy conservation for inner city, young, underemployed people, and the others in Fredricksburg, Maryland and in DC with the still-new Solar Lobby.

After having sat with renewable energy guru Amory Lovins in a two-day intensive seminar in the fall of 1977 then devouring his seminal book "Soft Energy Paths" and work-

ing on the consulting and academic side of energy conservation, I just had to take the Memphis job.

The chance to implement the solar systems hands-on,
working in a community to build the jobs and economic
development that Amory promised would come along with
renewable energy was unique. Can this work? I wanted to
be part of the experiment. Solar was rising nationally, and
America was the world's leader in flat-plate collector production. That forty percent federal tax credit had worked
some considerable magic.

The New Memphis Development Corporation got two
million Federal dollars over three years from a surprising
but effective national alliance between the new Department
of Energy, the Department of Labor and Community Services Administration—the anti-poverty agency. They hired
me and a local black college-educated Viet Nam veteran
and construction foreman Lee Cummings, who also taught
math in prison at night to supplement his income. We were
the only interviewees. I was the only white man in the company.

We were one of fifteen of these solar/job/economic development demonstration programs around the country
everywhere from the Chippewa Cree Indian reservation in
Montana, to the South Bronx, west Texas and impoverished
communities all over the country. Most of the program leaders were far more experienced in design and community organization than I was, but some of the leadership at New
Memphis had really been around politically and knew how
to make it rain in Tennessee. We had a lot of latitude; no one
had done this before, there was no template. That became a
subtheme of my career.

I spent the next three years in a black economic development organization, leading young, mostly black, mostly male trainees through a sixteen-week intensive course in solar, conservation, building and installing solar hot water and greenhouses.

The idea was the trainees would all come out of this blitz course ready for work in the solar industry that was booming nationally—we were still getting quite a political energy lift from Carter's energy policies and the second oil embargo. There were solar hot water panels on the White House, and the Tennessee Valley Authority also chipped in locally, financing 1,000 solar water heaters. TVA Chairman David Freeman had declared renewable energy the way forward. The solar installers for the 1,000 were supposed to hire our trainees and that was to jump start the industry. It didn't really work out that way very often. They hired their own, and energy prices were too cheap to make it pay, plus Reagan nixed the solar tax credit and took the panels off the White House.

After three years, the Feds pulled the plug on us all. Of our seventy trainees I counted 35 having had what I'd call a good outcome, including full-time employment, marrying or joining the Army. But we installed 50 solar water heaters and built ten attached solar greenhouses for low-income people around Memphis and made the front page of the metro section of the Commercial Appeal a couple of times. Renewables were, it seemed, gaining traction.

After a year of house-painting, consulting, travel and starting a massage practice, I got a phone call from my old boss at Integrated Energy Systems, now simply IES Engineers. "Pollock," as Dan addressed me, "I've got an interesting new project that would suit you—building and running a training program for local government energy officers (LEOs) and then proving they can earn their salary in electricity conservation savings or the utilities will reimburse the governments that hired them." I joined right up and returned to Chapel Hill with my then-partner and her son in tow.

For the next four years, from 1983 through '87, I developed and ran the LEO program, training seventeen energy conservation specialists representing 31 governments in accounting for building energy consumption, identifying and implementing savings opportunities and helping them calculate the paybacks. No one had done a similar thing anywhere in the nation. We were so successful that only one of the 31 governments was able to claim that they didn't make back all of the salary they'd paid the LEO over two years. During those years, our firm also conducted energy audits for everyone from Fort Knox to Bojangles.

While I toiled for IES Engineers, in 1984, the Town of Chapel Hill and Orange County tried to buy land adjoining both their landfill and a long established rural minority neighborhood to expand the existing landfill. A furor arose; I wandered down to the public hearing and spoke rationally amidst the noise and heat about the alternatives they might pursue and soon after found myself chairing Orange County's first Solid Waste Task Force, established later that year. We spent two years stumbling towards alternative solutions. Our final report to the County said that Orange County and its towns should have an open landfill site search process, consider alternative technologies, and begin a waste reduction and recycling program.

Little did I know in helping write the report, I'd written my own ticket. Shortly after its submittal, a friend inside the Town of Chapel Hill local government called and said, "Blair, I can't believe you're not applying for that job." "Which job is that?" I asked naively. Well it turns out the elected bodies took the report seriously and suddenly decided they wanted to start a recycling program and needed someone to run it. Right around that time, they had a landfill study which said they had only ten years of capacity left. Game on.

I knew little about recycling, but knew I was bored with energy conservation consulting. I was not an engineer, few projects we'd recommended had gotten built and the company direction was changing from consultation to design. Though I'd begun to prosper a bit, it was time for something else. So I interviewed and got the new job. Again, as I found out later, I was the only interviewee. At that time, I was also splitting from my partner and buying my first house, a fixer-upper complete with a rotting bathroom and kitchen floors.

Now twenty-five years later, the recycling program in Orange County is second to none in the State and is acknowledged internationally. Newly minted environmental bureaucrats from Kazakhstan and Kosovo have toured our facilities and heard the spiel. I can't claim credit for all our great success, but as a program innovator and builder I was out leading the charge with great local support from the beginning. Our program has won the National Recycling Coalition's award for best municipal public education program and the Carolina Recycling Association's awards for best urban recycling and best hazardous household waste programs. In 2011 I was voted best online recycling instructor for the Solid Waste Association of North America's recycling manager training course.

Long-entrenched bureaucrats surreptitiously bet against me; my boss told me later they'd said upon seeing me in action, "Pollock won't last six months." Instead I found partners and allies in the community and bosses who tolerated my idiosyncrasies, because I got things done. I had very little idea of how to set up or promote a recycling program, but it's certainly not rocket science. I made a lot of calls to other recyclers and plenty of mistakes. I cut myself more than once drilling holes and putting chains on aluminum recycling bin lids to prevent theft.

Early on I rode a lot of midnight routes with our recycled cardboard collector, jaw boned with bar owners so they'd start sorting glass into three different bins by color as programs then required, got money to advertise our programs (a thing that was unheard of for governments at that time), recruited neighborhood recycling block captains by hanging out at recycling drop off sites, and basically did a lot of street-level organizing. Everyone said "yes."

Much of this work was building relationships either inside the government or in the community, ultimately creating a cultural expectation that there would be recycling everywhere. After two years I had a community educator and curbside recycling. In two more years a collector for bar glass and a commercial and apartment program manager. After the tenth year, it became obvious we were here to stay. The program is now almost fifty percent of Orange County's Solid Waste operation.

Granted, Chapel Hill and the County generally was a very welcoming pond to swim in, but without programmatic success, working closely with the media, having elected officials bask in the programs' reflected light, good financing from, ironically, the landfill's income, and great popularity, I would have achieved nothing. It's a balance between being brave enough to try things and not too bold or bombastic about it. I was also quite lucky to consistently work for people who gave me lots of room to maneuver, fail, innovate, stumble and do more. I guess they realized I was committed and, of course, I should be.

Elaine Chiosso

In our town Elaine is an institution. She is an environmentalist who founded the Haw River Assembly, and has been fighting on behalf of the Haw River for what seems like forever.

Every parent with a child in Chatham County schools has a relationship to the Haw River Assembly, which has exposed thousands of kids to the flora and fauna of the Haw River. Elaine's reach is vast, and I'm guessing it might be "unexpectedly so."

One of the boundaries of our property is Stinking Creek. It gets its name from the wood bison that once inhabited these forests, and were slaughtered to extinction by settlers. They used to throw the carcasses onto giant piles, which would decompose, and stink. Stinking Creek feeds into Jordan Lake, which is the drinking supply for the Town of Cary, and as such it falls into the domain of the Haw River Assembly.

When they asked me to join their "stream stewardship" program, to monitor water quality throughout the year, I agreed. They gave us a net, and some training, and we spent some time splashing around in the creek and counting mayfly larvae and crayfish, and turning over rocks to inspect for various aquatic life.

As a "Stream Steward" I learned a lot about clean water. And I realized Elaine's organization wasn't just a bunch of aging hippies. My respect for her went up several notches.

And with time I watched her organization win some grants, and professionalize, and become a force to be reckoned with. I would occasionally find myself at Town Hall for a rezoning hearing, and I noticed Elaine, or someone from her organization was always present.

And I noticed how the town fathers would refer to her condescendingly as "our favorite environmentalist."

Elaine holds power. She has a vast membership, she has vast experience, she has a hook into the hearts and minds of thousands of school children. As clean water moves to the forefront of the environmental movement, and as its importance becomes increasingly understood, Elaine and her work are on the vanguard of societal change.

Here is her story…

SHE SPEAKS FOR THE RIVER

Elaine Chiosso.

I was born in the middle of the 20th century on the western edge of our country, near the Pacific Ocean. I have always loved water, whether it was running through storm puddles on rainy days, playing in creeks, or braving the cold ocean waters. Water speaks to me in a deep way, and for many years now, my work has been to speak for the river where I live in the Piedmont of North Carolina. As the Haw River keeper for the Haw River Assembly, I defend the river and advocate for clean water for all the communities that depend on the river for life. The Haw River watershed, with a 110-mile river running through 8 counties and forming Jordan Lake, is home to about 900,000 residents, and provides drinking water and recreation to the Triangle and Triad regions. Protecting this large watershed, which is under constant and serious threat from rapid development and urbanization, has been my life work for 17 years.

I make sure the issues that threaten the waters of the Haw River are heard: when impacts such as development or industry threaten water quality, when public policy must be strengthened to protect water, and when citizens and communities are struggling to protect clean water in their own communities. Organizing citizen activists for public hearings and for Clean Water Lobby Days at the legislature in Raleigh, flying up the river with a volunteer pilot to track sediment from new construction projects, and out on the river or creeks taking water samples to investigate pollution—these are the more exciting parts of my work. Not so exciting is the constant effort needed to raise funds to keep this work going, or the very slow effort of pushing for better regulations and enforcement that are needed to keep water clean.

Protecting the Haw watershed is an important part of a larger cause that has driven me for most of my life—the need to speak out about injustices against our earth and its people. I have been a community activist working for protection of the environment and for social justice since I was a teenager. I could not sit by when bad things were happening around me, and was drawn into the big issues of the day—protesting the Vietnam war, volunteering to clean up (rather futilely) a coastal oil spill, and working with inner city kids who needed a place to play in the summer.

Growing up near San Francisco, I watched as the agricultural land around us was bought by developers who crowded houses on small lots up to the edge of the cliffs along the Pacific (some later fell in!). I watched as the hillsides my friends and I played on were paved over. A lovely little creek I played in near my grandmother's house in the summertime was a place of mystery and delight as we waded through dappled sunlight and little fish. One summer I returned to see it gone—channeled into a concrete canal to carry away storm water from a new freeway. My heart was broken. In a high school civics class I learned, from an extraordinary teacher, that you could search county records to see the connection between developers' interests—changing zoning laws—and their campaign contributions to candidates that would follow those interests. It was a lesson I never forgot.

When I moved to North Carolina in 1971, I fell in love with its forests, creeks, and the Haw River. I fell in love with the generosity and kindness of the people here too, people of all kinds who could see beyond this radical, Italian-American kid from California with her ideas of organic gardening and living "off-grid." I soon found myself in the thick of a local campaign to successfully elect the first African American to the Board of the County Commissioners since Reconstruction, and a few years later, to help elect the first woman to that same Board. I was determined to protect the natural beauty I discovered here from the fate of my own childhood places. I found myself standing up against powerful interests who wanted to build a hazardous waste incinerator; a dump for PCB's in an African-American neighborhood; and poorly planned development projects that would send mud into creeks. I graduated with a B.S. degree in Science Education from UNC-Chapel Hill and have used it to bring issues of environmental concern to the public. I worked at RAFI in the 1980's on crop genetic resources issues with Cary Fowler, who has gone on to help create the world's new seed bank in Norway. During that time my former husband and I opened our house and hearts to Victor Montejo, a Mayan teacher and writer who had escaped from the repressive regime in Guatemala. He lived with us for several months before his wife and children could join him and he began a university and literary career that took him to a faculty position at the University of California at Davis. He is now the Minister of Peace in Guatemala.

Becoming involved in the Haw River Assembly when it was founded in 1982 was a natural for me. The Haw River Assembly is a grassroots organization working to protect the Haw River and Jordan Lake, and to build a community that supports this vision. I served as a Board member, President, and in 1998, became its first Executive Director. In 2008 the Haw River Assembly became a licensed Waterkeeper program and I became the new Haw Riverkeeper. Under my leadership, the Haw River Assembly has greatly expanded its programs, which involve other staff, members and hundreds of volunteers. Their efforts and partnership in this work are invaluable, and I have learned much through them. Together we have learned that our voices and actions can be powerful, even if we have too few dollars and resources to support us at times. We have built impressive and creative programs including the largest citizen water-monitoring program in the state, and the annual Haw River Learning Celebration river field trip takes fourth-graders throughout the watershed. Renowned for its excellence and now in its 23rd year, the Learning Celebration has reached over 38,000 schoolchildren from all racial and socio-economic groups since its inception. I understand the importance of balancing the fight for environmental protection with the deep need to nurture our sense of wonder and love for the natural world. Without that love, this work would be hard to sustain. My goal is to always empower others, and be empowered by them, so that together we can stand firm even when it seems hopeless. We experience strength in numbers when working together, and see and celebrate the value of winning small victories and moving forward one step at a time.

In this work as a "voice for the river," I have not hesitated to challenge those who would degrade the river, including large-scale developers, or municipalities reluctant to do what it takes to protect surface waters, to upgrade wastewater treatment plants needing improvement, and fix polluting industries. I know I have made enemies, and there have been a few times driving home alone at night after a particularly embattled public hearing that I wondered if I was being followed. Not paranoia, but a wariness that comes from knowing your insistence on environmental protection is costing developers money. A long history of doing what's right for the planet, and becoming more knowledgeable along the way has its rewards too.

I sometimes joke that I just never really left college; given all the new information I've had to learn to do this work. I've been asked to serve on many regional and state commissions and boards including the N.C. Rivers Assessment Advisory Board, the Jordan Lake Stakeholder Project for new state rules to reduce pollution, and the Coalition to pass the Drinking Water Reservoir Protection Act in 2005. I was appointed by Governor Hunt to the State Infrastructure Council (1999-2001) and by Governor Easley to the N.C. Sedimentation Control Commission in 2006 and again in 2008—the only woman member at that time. I worked for seven years to get state rules passed to reduce pollution in Jordan Lake, often as the sole voice speaking for clean water.

This work can be lonely sometimes, and the money interests and power are usually on the other side of these issues. Support from co-workers, board members, and the larger community make the work possible, sustainable and always interesting. Successes in this work are few and hard won, but without our efforts the river, and people's lives, would surely be worse off.

Over the years, I've chosen a life of activist work over a more financially rewarding career, which has sometimes meant cars that don't start on a winter morning, or figuring out which bills could be paid the next month. The work took a toll on my personal life as well, and after divorce, as a single mother of two daughters, I faced the difficult challenges of balancing family life with this work of community activism and protecting the environment. But I also chose a life of rich community and where my children could grow up playing in the wilds of the forest and swimming in the beautiful creek nearby. I've loved this life of watching the landscape change through the seasons, and that has fed my efforts to protect it from bulldozers. I hope my two now-grown daughters see me as a strong, but compassionate woman, as my own mother was in her lifetime.

Protecting the Haw River and Jordan Lake are a passionate concern because I care about the community that lives in this watershed. Clean streams and drinking water are everyone's issues, and I believe that we are most successful when we find ways to reach out beyond our comfort zone to find common ground with others. To this end, I fostered partnerships at HRA with groups such as the West End Revitalization Association, working for "Rights to Basic Amenities" including clean water in Mebane's African American communities; and the GASP group in Alamance County, working to stop pollution from the Stericycle medical waste incinerator. I'm working on initiatives to make the Haw

River Assembly an organization that better represents the diversity of the whole population in our watershed, and more relevant to all communities.

People sometimes ask how I keep doing this work—what keeps me going? Well, I just can't stand by and see injustice being done, whether to people or to the river. Working with others to protect our natural world brings me new strength. Watching the ospreys build their nests at Jordan Lake each spring and herons fishing in the river; watching children playing in streams where clean water flows; and listening to the sound of water flowing over rocks on its journey to the sea, and singing songs with others about these beautiful parts of our world—this keeps me going. My advice to others is: Raise your voices. Be witnesses. Speak truth to those with power. All our voices count. And always, always get out there and enjoy the beauty of the world, and be renewed by it.

Albert Bates

I first met Albert Bates in Puyllup, Washington, at the Mother Earth News Fair. I bumped into him accidentally; he was standing against the back wall of a solar presentation in which all the seats were filled. I slipped in and stood next to him, and I recognized him.

My problem was that I was an Albert Bates fan. I had read his essays about The Farm, and I had read his articles in *Permaculture Activist*, and like any good fan, I was at a loss for words.

I leaned over and said, "You're Albert Bates?"

"Yup."

"I think I've been reading your work for 27 years."

"Could be," he replied.

We stood next to each other for awhile as the presenter carried on.

I leaned his way and said, "Are you getting anything new out of this?"

"Nope," was his reply.

"Do you want to go talk?"

"Sure," he said, and the two of us broke away to the speaker's green room.

Basically my task was to not slobber on my hero. And he was largely indifferent. Biodiesel didn't interest him. And there was nothing I could tell him about community, or sustainability, or environmentalism, or anything, so it seemed. As a rabid fan, I believe I simply bored him.

Luckily at one point he said, "What do you know about plastics to oil?" That was a subject I had accidentally studied—I knew a lot about plastics to oil.

That's all Albert wanted. When I started going through the numbers on plastics to oil conversion I shifted from being just another drooling fan to someone he could learn from, and when that happened we decided to go for a beer.

When it came time to find a place for a beer we found ourselves trudging through sprawl America, with no sidewalks, across pesticide laden lawns, to an Olive Garden restaurant.

I was both stunned and disheartened. On the one hand I was having a beer with the grandfather of permaculture, my hero, Albert Bates. On the other we were in an Olive Garden.

We have stayed in touch since then, and when I asked him to contribute to this book, he sent me a youtube video of an extemporaneous talk which he gave at the 2011 *International Conference on Sustainability, Transition and Culture Change: Vision, Action Leadership* in Traverse City, Michigan.

I tried my best to watch Albert's speech on the screen and to type it into a file, but I was hopeless on that front, so I hired a graduate student. I then took a crack at editing it, and Albert took a turn at rewriting it, and here it is…

FINDING THE OTHERS

Albert Bates

I was born in Hawaii, grew up in Connecticut, and went to Syracuse University, then law school. After graduation in 1972 I hiked the Appalachian Trail, to get out of the city and back to fresh air and sanity for a while before going on into whatever career I would likely follow. I'd had a number of offers with attractive starting salaries in the six digit range. I got down into Tennessee, got off the trail for a while, and stopped to visit The Farm, which was just then getting started as a rural, hippie, experimental commune. I fell into that counterculture, was sucked into its gravity field and never escaped.

For the next 40 years, and still today, I am pursuing the original vision I came into contact with there—of self sufficiency, self reliance, healthy babies, clean air, and also making a positive contribution; making the world consistently a little better for generations still to come.

I was not somebody you might expect to drop out of conventional society. I grew up in wealthy white-bread Connecticut, where my high school sport was equestrian three-day eventing—dressage, stadium jumping and outdoor

courses. At The Farm I learned to train horses in a different way, getting them to pull plows, cultivators and heavy
wagons.

At The Farm I developed many skills. You could pretty
much learn to do whatever you wanted, but one gravitated
towards things that were most needed. So if no one was
doing sewage treatment, that was an opportunity for some
young person to step up and create a constructed wetlands,
or design a better composting toilet, or build a methane di-
gester, something along those lines. It was an exciting time.
I became a stonemason. I hand painted signs for buildings.
I illustrated manuscripts in the art department of our printing company. I learned to be a typesetter, working with a
very early version of MS-DOS to hook dumb-terminals to a
CPU and connect a word-processor to a linotyper. I drove an
ambulance and became a licensed EMT. I became a scrapper
and took down a huge flour mill in Viola, Tennessee and
a granary in Pulaski, and rebuilt them back at The Farm,
where I milled flour, about a ton a day. I also made grits,
groats, horse feed, soy nuts, soy coffee and peanut butter.

As we built our village, any profession you could name
fell into the category of "immediate opportunities available,
no experience needed." You got up in the morning. You went
to work. But work was saving the world, and it was doing
it by exploring all these old crafts and trades and the occasional new one.

As a law school graduate, I found myself living in a community that had little use for lawyers. For most of my first
seven years at The Farm I didn't do any legal work at all.
I was a flour miller and a horse trainer. But then the nuke
arrived in our neighborhood. The Tennessee Valley Author-

ity (TVA) had an ambitious plan to build 20 nuclear power plants including a breeder reactor. So I was pulled out of early retirement and returned to my legal career. We stopped TVA in its tracks for a while. At one point, I personally was costing TVA six million dollars per day. I took the fight over nuclear power national and sued to shut down 190 facilities. I took at least four of those cases to the US Supreme Court, and argued before 20 federal appellate judges on various constitutional rights issues related to radiation and human health.

I didn't stop them. My argument, which was a moral argument about killing future children every time you turn on a light switch, really didn't persuade them. The antinuclear movement didn't stop nuclear construction in the United States. What stopped it was the economics. When S. David Freeman was appointed to head the TVA, he became the first utility CEO to ferret out what it actually cost to build, operate and eventually decommission nuclear power plants. Once that was known—all that red ink on TVA's balance sheets—the contract cancellations became an avalanche.

Our legal and moral argument boiled down to, simply, that your children and grandchildren and great grandchildren have the same inherent rights you do. These rights include the right to be natural—to not be genetically modified; to not be forced to inhale man-made toxic poisons in our air, or to drink them in our water; to not have to suffer birth defects and cancers and things carelessly heaped upon innocents by transgenerational tortfeasors.

Because of my experience with nuclear power and health, and because we also won the first successful claim at the Veterans Administration (VA) for exposure to Agent Orange,

I started getting requests for counsel from atomic veterans. At that time veterans were not allowed to pay lawyers to help with injury claims, so I decided just to represent them for free, since any other services they were provided were not adequate in such complex claims. By the early 1980s, I had the most clients of any private attorney for atomic veterans—and I reviewed more than 700 VA case files.

One of my clients was John Smitherman. He was aboard the battleship Nevada that was at the Crossroads tests in 1946. After the test the sailors went back on board and scrubbed the Nevada down to get it running again. The Nevada was the only ship berthed on Battleship Row to get underway and engage the enemy during Pearl Harbor. It had a crackerjack crew. Those guys died of cancer. They died of horrible diseases, like leukemia. Many died bleeding from every orifice.

John Smitherman had little black marks on the side of his legs from exposure to radiation. Those eventually developed into an edema, a swelling, and both of his legs were amputated. He didn't want his arms amputated when it spread up there, so he just put tourniquets on, tried to stop the swelling down into his hands. He knew that as soon as he let it go that he was going to lose his arms. And that's how he died.

There were a lot of guys like that, thousands, maybe more than died in the Pearl Harbor attack. I sat by John Smitherman's bedside when he passed away. And I feel like that experience gave me the right to become a voice for those men. I took those experiences very personally. Those men can't be here to speak for themselves anymore, but I'm here. I speak for them. And when I speak to an audience, or I go address schoolchildren, or I get into an argument with some ass about this stuff, like Stewart Brand, Mark Lynas, or James Lovelock, I get a little emotional. But I'm not speaking for myself. I'm those men's voice now.

I feel you can carry emotion to the point where it does some good, but then you can carry it too far. So I try to also be rational and logical about this sort of thing. From straight scientific proofs I can say that we are probably killing more people now with airport security screening machines than died on 9-11. I can't even begin to think about what is happening now in Japan, and for the next several generations there, and really, the environment has no borders.

I can't predict where the next disaster will come, only that it will, as surely as night follows day. TVA proposed 20 nuclear power plants, and more than half were cancelled and scrapped, but they've now become zombie nukes. The Obama administration wants to reanimate them.

I confess I'm more of a carrot person than a stick person. I like to hold out solutions; to say there are alternatives to this madness that are smarter, better, more cost efficient, and so forth. The concentrating photovoltaic arrays that I built for the World's Fair in '82, showed that you could run a solar array on 30% of ambient light and get 100% power by using simple cheap reflectors. That put the lie to some popular nonsense about solar power being useless on rainy days. We had a solar powered car that we ran through the World's Fair grounds to show you could quit fossil fuels cold. We actually rescued an old Victorian house in Knoxville when they were clearing the World's Fair site, and turned it into the Appropriate Community Technology Pavilion and had all kinds of new devices and ideas for better living on display there.

Showing people is very important—people often learn more from seeing and feeling and touching and getting to ride in a solar-powered car than they would ever get by reading about it or hearing the problem retold, over and over.

A local judge appointed me to handle an indigent case for a man caught robbing a liquor store that seems to keep coming up in the news today. We plea bargained the case and he served his sentence, but he lost his right to vote. Black people were disproportionately disenfranchised by that law, so I took it up on federal appeal under the Voting Rights Act. That was one we lost, but should have won. The Voting Rights Act is an "effects" test, not a legislative powers test, and eventually Congress or the courts will have to recognize that and correct it, nationally. I took a second case up under the Tennessee Constitution and won at our Supreme Court, restoring the rights of more than 200,000 Tennessee felons.

One of the projects that came across my desk when I was doing the lawyer thing was a nearby chemical company that was injecting their wastes into the ground. These were the residues from the production of agrochemicals like phosphates—organophosphates—and they were going into the local aquifer, which was a fresh water drinking source. These were the neurotoxins that came from bad batches of pesticides and herbicides, things that are toxic down into parts per trillion. They pressure-injected more than a billion gallons in Tennessee. We were saying "Hey, haven't you read the Safe Drinking Water Act? You're not allowed to do that."

And they were saying, "Tennessee has so much surface water, so many rivers and lakes here, you don't need that. You don't need water that deep."

And so we said, "What about population growth?"

"What about climate change?" And so, back in 1980, I had to go to court and convince a judge that climate change was going to be a game changer in middle Tennessee in a few years. I had to find experts and get special scientific evidence of various kinds. I got working with my congressman, a young guy named Al Gore, and he would drag agencies for reports, and give them to me. We started publicizing what was going on, as well as taking it into court. Gore held hearings and started talking about it in town meetings back home. Eventually, we were able to get laws passed in Tennessee that prohibited deep well injection, and now today prohibit hydraulic fracturing for natural gas. We were less successful with global warming.

Back in that period of time, the 1980s, we saw actual climate change happening around us. The climate that today exists at The Farm is completely different from the climate that existed when we arrived in 1970. When The Farm started in 1970, the climate it had then is now up near Lexington, Kentucky. The climate that we have today was down near Neshoba County, Mississippi. We know this from phenological studies; when the seasons change, when migrations happen, when flowers come into bloom, when the leaves change, and so forth. We watched climate move northward from 40 miles per decade in the 1970s to about 70 miles per decade now.

The fastest runner in the tree kingdom is spruce. It ran about 700 miles per century after the last Ice Age. It's the fastest tree migration that we know of. That's the speed that this change is happening in Tennessee right now. We don't know of any Southern trees that can move that fast. We've changed two USDA planting zones in 40 years. We are losing maples. I just saw my first cow killer ant, from Texas. We've had armadillos for 3 or 4 years now. If that's not obvious, I don't know what is. It's happening before our very eyes.

I gathered all of this into a book, called *Climate in Crisis* with a foreword by then Senator Gore. It told this story, but it also really kind of changed my outlook. I was ranting to judges and audiences on this whole thing about nuclear and chemical waste and natural rights, and really this...this is a bigger picture. Climate change is an existential question. When you begin to look at the studies, and you take them out beyond just the next 50 years, beyond the next 100 years, beyond 200 or 300 years, and you look at the accelerating rates of change, it's scary.

You start to look at things like clathrates bubbling in the Arctic now. They're sending a joint expedition from the National Academy of Sciences and its Russian counterpart out into the Arctic now, to try to measure the rate of clathrate release. It looks to be about the same as 50 million years ago, and if that's the case we can expect mid-continental temperatures within another century or two to average around 140–150 degrees in mid-summer. No forests can survive that. Can humans survive without forests? This is existential.

In human history we've never had the rates of climate change we have now. We didn't evolve with this. We evolved in the comfortable Holocene. What's our window of opportunity to fix this problem? If you ask our political leaders they will say the changes are so slow, it's multigenerational, we don't have to worry about it in our generation. We can take care of other issues first.

That's false. The window of opportunity to actually change and create a different future is very narrow, and we don't even know if it's still open. It may have closed before I was born, in 1947. How about that? And maybe, what I'm doing is just, you know, nothing. Maybe all of this is just a useless exercise.

For the past few years I have been going to the Association for the Study of Peak Oil's conferences. When I was at the one in Houston a few years ago, 2006 I think it was, I had this moment that I call my "Houston Moment." It's not like "Houston we have a problem," It was that I was in Houston and had this realization that it's fucked. We may have already screwed it up so bad that we can't get it back. And I don't know if any of the things I've spent my life doing—writing books, going out on tour, talking, meeting with people, trying to raise consciousness—are going to have any effect at all. And I look at all the good things The Farm has done, and all the things we've done in terms of solar power installation and ecovillage ideas, and today that solar power installation seems like fairy dust to me, because it's like a techno-fix on this much larger picture of how humans relate to the natural environment.

And I worry about how much time we spend on strategies like politics. I attended the Keystone Pipeline protest at the White House and Bill McKibben was really pushing hard on "get involved with the election, get involved with Obama, force Obama to do what he promised to do, try to get the politicians to move in the right direction after they make their pledges," and I really look at all that and say "We're being played, you know? That's a game, that's not necessarily doing what it's purporting to do."

And really, what's out there now is this kind of crazy, mad-hatter world of politics that's totally divorced from reality, and do we really want to play that game? Do we really want to be engaged with those folks? Scientists are looking at the climate crisis and they're calling it a "hyperwicked problem." This is just a technical way of saying that there are complex interrelationships in a matrix of causes that defies resolution using normal problem-solving mechanisms. What we really need to do is think more in new, comprehensive, holistic ways that take account of all of these other dimensions, including our own neurobiology.

Confirmation bias is when you're in your own little cocoon or bubble of how you think. You like to hear other people confirm that what you've decided on is great, and so you take your RSS feeds and you choose the *Wall Street Journal* or the *New York Times*, and you listen to Rush Limbaugh or Bill Maher, and you come to conferences because they reinforce what you already believe. But if you understand confirmation bias, you have to wonder, is our thing just a kind of a box? Are we in a box? Have we made our own sounding board, and we're just sort of hearing our own echo all the time? And are we deluding ourselves?

Another kind of bias is normalcy bias, which is, you really want it to be normal, so you tune out and ignore things that are too disruptive of your normalcy. The building may be on fire, but you're bantering with someone, or talking on the phone, because you really don't want that fire. These are things we're starting to learn about our own neurological make-up.

When I look at some of the messages coming out of the Occupy movement I feel very hopeful. Their process is very good. At the same time, there's so much of the big picture that I have come to understand over 40 years that they're not yet seeing. And, really, there are demands being placed on society that society may not be able to meet. There are hyperwicked problems like the energy picture, and peak everything, the overdraft on planetary resources, and our collective response is not to tackle the problems head-on, or develop some new holistic disciplines to create hypersolutions, but just to express a lot of frustration. To quibble over the symptoms, like the street riots in Greece or the farmers' protests in France.

When I was at Occupy New York, Jan Lundberg raised his voice in the meeting and said, "I propose, as a goal, the 20 hour work week. Okay?" And so the group started talking about that. And the obvious questions come up. "Well, how am I going to pay my rent?" "How are we going to put food on the table if we can barely do it now?"

My thinking on that is which is more valuable? Time or money? It's really about what you can do with time. You can grow food. You can make things. You can become more self-reliant. If you can scale back your dependency on money, and make that smaller, that's the direction that you need to go.

We tend to solve a problem and then solve the next problem based on our first solution. It's Severeid's Law. The cause of all problems is solutions. So we're moving one step at a time, all the time, in a very linear fashion. But actually Gaia is not structured linearly. She's a non-linear system. You jingle something over here, it jangles over there. And, you don't know how the connection happened, you don't know where the connection is, you can't see it. But, it's connected.

So what's the non-linear brain? The non-linear brain is the collected intelligence of all other living species. Everything from bacteria up to higher life forms. Each of them with a unique way of processing, and of recognizing and seeing patterns and responding and relating to them and to each other, and all of that is being now replaced by one creature. Homo. And so we are co-opting, we are taking all the protoplasm, and consolidating it, and all the brain processing power of Gaia is being lobotomized, and taken down to this one small piece of the brain, which is linear. Scary.

I recently read a paper that was speculating about how the little Ice Age in Europe was in part caused by the reforestation of the Amazon and the Central America after the Columbian Encounter. It took so much carbon out of the atmosphere it froze Europe. Now they're looking at lake sediments and they're figuring out that the population explosion in the Americas during that monumental architecture period was actually taking so much carbon and putting it into the atmosphere while they were making lime for their cities that they caused the Medieval Maximum, the warming period that drove the Moors into Spain. And so while climate deniers like Lord Monkton and James Inhofe are fond of pointing to the Medieval Maximum and saying that between 700 and 1100 AD we had this warming period, and that was not man made, actually, maybe it was. Maybe it was man made. Which means there's a huge sensitivity here, between human activity and the global climate. If you stand on the moon and look back at the earth, there are two things you can see with the naked eye that are man made. One is the Sahara Desert. The other is the Amazon Rainforest. Which would you rather we were making?

The Native American wisdom of revering the earth, and not scarring her to take out uranium and coal, and all of that praying towards the animals before you kill them, and things like that, has a real world impact, and a real world effect. Because we're all connected in that way, integrally interwoven with this larger system, in ways that we barely understand. We can see that we're now at these terminal crisis points of climate change with various chemicals and ocean acidification and other kinds of warnings. And we can make our own threat matrix of things that are challenging to us, and areas that we need to be concerned about, and areas that we can worry about, but I think this whole idea of the profound connection is lost in our culture. How profoundly connected we are with the natural world, and each other, and with all our relations. Every little thing we do has some butterfly effect.

It reminds me of the Richard Dreyfus character in *Close Encounters of the Third Kind*. He was sitting at the dinner table making a mesa out of his mashed potatoes. He looks up, and his wife, played by Teri Garr, is sitting across this dinner table staring at him, and his kids are sitting staring at him, and he's like, just making this mashed potato mountain because his subconscious is telling him to do this. And it turns out there are other people having the same process, elsewhere. They all have a shared vision. And what he really needs to do is find the others. That's the message. Find the others. So really what we're doing here, and our only hope in this, is finding the others.

Jennifer Radtke

I have long bumped into Jennifer at grassroots biodiesel conferences. As a creator of Biofuels Oasis in Berkeley, she is a legend.

I once read her remarkable, *Not a Gas Station* on a long plane ride home from California, and it completely inspired me. I loved it. It made me want to open a business. Then I remembered I already had a business that needed attention.

The day I finally had a chance to go to lunch with Jennifer I was already in San Francisco at a Slow Money conference. I caught a subway to Berkeley and walked over to Biofuels Oasis. Jennifer was finishing her shift and invited me to join her. Apparently it was her turn to deal with the litter about the place. She donned rubber gloves and went about the task of picking up the debris of urban life that had encroached upon her fueling station.

When she was finished with the trash we walked over to a vegan Mexican joint that she liked so that she could get her favorite meal. I outlined the concept of *Small Stories, Big Changes* and asked her to contribute. She had made a promise to herself to not take on any more projects until the end of the year, but figured if I could extend the deadline a bit she could make an exception.

Here is Jennifer's take on the subject...

RIDING THE DEMON

Jennifer Radtke

In the midst of the trying permitting process for our new biodiesel station, I had a dream. I was riding on the back of an eagle but instead of majestically soaring, the eagle was flying me around in daredevil circles over and over again. The eagle said, "Get used to this and have fun!" I remembered as a kid riding the Demon at Great America north of Chicago which took you in two corkscrew turns upside down. I also loved the Eagle rollercoaster which had one huge drop which made everyone scream as you lifted your arms and felt as if you were falling for seconds on end. After riding, my friend and I would get back in line to do it again and again. Riding rollercoasters was unknowingly my training ground for running a cutting-edge activist business. The dream was a great reminder that I can enjoy and have fun during the intense combination of fear and exhilaration.

The permitting process kept going, extending out to more than two years. Our zoning permit was approved but the City bureaucrats rejected our building permit a third time and gave us more corrections. I was mired in depression. Maybe we were beaten and would never get approved.

At the same time, my cat disappeared. She simply didn't come home one night. Immediately I assumed she was dead. I had been well-trained growing up in worse-case scenario thinking: when in doubt, always jump to the worst-case conclusion. I did that quickly here. I cried and cried and mourned her. On the third day, I decided to walk around the neighborhood and ask if people had seen her. I knocked on neighbors doors. Every single one told me a story about how their cat had disappeared for weeks or months, but had returned. That night I decided to believe. I decided to believe that my cat was well and alive and would return. The next morning I was talking on the phone to the architects about the building permit and I heard a noise. I looked and my cat was back and hungrily eating her food. I was so happy I exclaimed and she meowed in response. We have never been apart again.

Doubts continue to come up for me, but after this episode of facing it and getting down and dirty with it, now I have an antidote. I make up a mantra with "I believe…", repeat it, and believe deep inside my bones. During these periods of doubt, I also read stories of people who have seemingly done the impossible. I have these collected for just these situations.

Not only did my cat return, but the building permit was approved on the third attempt with one remaining caveat. We could start to build, but the above-ground tank was still in question. They had engineering calculations that the tank was attached to its footing and would withstand earthquake forces, but they wanted calculations that the actual tank would withstand earthquake forces. The tank manufacturer was baffled (pun intended for those that know that tanks often have baffles), as they had never been asked this before. We started construction, but I continued to work on getting tank approval. Finally, the building department gave us some specific specs from a tank standard that we had to meet.

I went on a hike up along the ridges of the Oakland hills, which puts me up so high that I not only can touch the sky but can look down at it. Being in the sky makes me feel like anything is possible; ideas and perspectives pop into my mind that I couldn't see down at ocean level.

I remembered something seemingly from a past life it seemed so distant, but actually was only a few years ago, when we got the original station approved. The fire department gave us a code section they interpreted one way. I read the code section, wrote up an opinion of it that agreed with our position, paid a fire consultant to sign the opinion, and we got approval. Hah, of course, the final step in our approval process would be the same this time and I knew exactly what to do. Finally, I could see the end in sight. It had been a long, arduous journey into the darkest night of doubt inside me and back out into the light of belief.

I sat down with the engineering code, wrote up a response to each section (some of the sections didn't apply to us because they were for cylindrical tanks and we had a rectangular tank), and got the tank engineer to sign it. The building department approved it just in time for us to install the tank.

Things seemed to happen just at the right time. There were many skills I learned long ago that suddenly were needed at a key moment, and then it finally makes sense why I learned them. People, funding, tools showed up just as we needed them. For example, a biodiesel customer came in and volunteered her services as a soil engineer. I didn't even know such an occupation existed and was sure we didn't need that for our building permit, but I took her name and number anyway. Months later we did indeed need a soil engineer and not only did I know what it was, but knew one that could help.

Sometimes it's the opposite, though, and it seems help isn't waiting in the wings. I used to hate it when I wouldn't get the housing situation or job I really wanted and people would say that it's because there is a more perfect one in the future for me. But the biodiesel business has dragged me kicking and screaming to the practice of patience. Even in simple things, the perfect thing may be sometime in the future. For the last six months I have been on the lookout for a storage cabinet for our bathroom, but could not find what I was looking for. I had about given up and suddenly my housemate had two cabinets in his truck which he had just removed from a house. The cabinets match the coloring of the biodiesel station bathroom like they had been picked out ahead of time. Now, when the thing I think I need isn't showing up, I have patience to wait and trust the process. When delays happen I may initially get frustrated, but I also look for opportunities in the slow-down.

Some people are addicted to drugs, some to TV, I'm addicted to work. It's an addiction that gets rewarded in our culture. And it is praised, which makes it harder to see it as an addiction. Addictions are things you do to avoid your life, avoid feeling your emotions, avoid being present. When I'm stressed about something in life, I work like crazy and think of nothing else.

Perhaps life loves us so much that if we don't learn a lesson the first time it will keep throwing us the lesson again. Life believes in us and knows we want to learn this lesson and are fully capable of learning it. I had been working on my workaholism for years, but hadn't quite gotten to the core of it. Life orchestrated the perfect trap for me and I fell right into it. I get all passionate about something (well usually about 10 different things) and terribly excited, plan a bunch of activities for the year, and realize in the middle that I'm too busy and it's no fun anymore. I'm committed and I push through and get burnt out. We expected the permitting process and construction for the new station to take less than a year. Instead it dragged on for two years. The rollercoaster ride of fear and extreme work took their toll and I went past my edge, beyond burn-out and into major adrenal fatigue.

In a dream I saw a picture of my adrenal glands. They were black and burnt to a crisp. I slept 12 hours a night and took naps during the day. The rest of the time I sat around. I worked three days a week and spent the other four days resting up in order that I could work again. I remember teaching a biodiesel class once when I was experiencing complete exhaustion. I felt like a cartoon character with toothpicks holding up my eyelids. Slowly, over three years, my energy built back up. When you push your energy so low, it takes years to recover. I am thankful that I surrendered to the process and the exhaustion. I made it a priority to rest, sleep, rest, and sleep some more.

Not having energy made me look at things differently. I learned that I can be the idea person, but don't need to carry out the ideas. As I enter my forties, I can be a mentor. I again can offer my wisdom, but don't need to work so hard. Work is taking on a different meaning. It's about inspiring, nurturing, facilitating, not physically doing.

Recently I attended a California biodiesel conference in San Francisco. Lots of people expressed appreciation to me personally for teaching them how to change their first fuel filter, for teaching a class years ago that got them started in biodiesel, and for writing my book about starting a biodiesel station, which they give to new employees to read. In the past, I would have brushed it all off with a "No Problem," as I was moving too fast, and on to the next class and thing that inspired me. But the adrenal fatigue has slowed me down to a different speed, and I could take in all the appreciation of my past work, really take it in deeply, so I can continue to teach and give to the next biodiesel generation.

My past ten years of being a biodiesel activist has not been lonely. It's been crowded with people. It started with the Berkeley Biodiesel Collective which was a volunteer group of 20–30 people. We always shared lots of yummy food when we got together and had lots of fun. There was a pioneering spirit in this group. Many of us also grew our own food and had backyard chickens; we were kindred spirits in taking action on what we believed in, and valuing having time to do the things that gave us joy over money. Many of us work part-time and live simply. I met many people then that are still my good friends today.

Out of the Berkeley Biodiesel Collective goodness, my business, the BioFuel Oasis biodiesel station, was born. Another woman and I co-founded and soon expanded to being a worker-owned cooperative of five women. A couple of people have come and gone, but we are still a co-op of five women. These women are like sisters to me and I am so glad to have them in my life and be in business with them. We have a lot of trust built up over the years and a solid way of making decisions.

I've told the permitting process from my personal perspective, but in no way did I do it alone. The new station was co-built and co-planned by five of us worker-owners at the BioFuel Oasis. I dreamed that I flew up to the top of a mountain. Athena, goddess of wisdom, courage, and just warfare, was there with the four other Oasis women. First we danced around an olive tree having fun and then we all stood in a line, equal, holding hands, and looking out into the future. Like Athena, we are all women warriors and fierce earth guardians working together.

I live with other people as well. Living and being in business with lots of people is unusual, but I can't imagine it any other way. I love having other people around. How lonely it would be for me to live by myself or own a business by myself. Part of the secret of happily collaborating closely, whether at home or work, with other people is to trust and believe that they care about me and my happiness. When someone's actions upset me, I often go to a place of doubt, thinking that they are doing it on purpose to upset me or with ulterior motives. Because I have many years of trust with my housemates and business sisters, I can transform that doubt quickly with my belief mantra. I trust that they care about me and will listen to my perspective and my needs. Speaking up and communicating each time builds more and more trust.

What I've created in my life is very much in line with my growing up. The family stories of my youth were empowering. My mom worked as a secretary for Milwaukee County and the supervisors instituted a new policy that all the secretaries needed to substitute for the receptionist and answer the phone. Everyone hated this. My mom went around gathering signatures from everyone in the department saying they wanted this changed. First, she got signatures from the most outspoken people and gathered the last signature from the most unwilling person who, when they saw everyone else had signed, signed too. With unanimous opposition to the policy, the supervisors had no choice but to change the policy.

My dad worked as an electrical engineer at a big factory. When I was about two, the factory workers went on strike. The factory management asked the engineers and other professional workers to do the factory work in order to break the strike. My dad refused, as he supported the union. He thought it disgusting that his fellow engineers were getting bonuses and overtime, and buying new cars, from working in the factory (they couldn't do the work as efficiently as the real workers so they got overtime). One Friday, management threatened that he would have to go work in the factory or lose his job. My dad researched the legalities over the weekend and concluded that they could fire him with no recourse. He told them he wouldn't work in the factory, expecting to be fired. Instead, they found him work to do outside the factory and kept him on.

Soon after, my dad quit and went to law school. He graduated in the top ten of his class, but instead of joining a law firm, he worked in criminal law defending poor people for over 20 years. In his 50s, he went back to school again. This time to medical school and became a doctor working first with the homeless and then in the emergency room with war veterans. My mom also went back to school in her 50s to get a master's in social work. She's worked in the foster care system, as a juvenile probation officer, and with kids with disabilities. Having retired, she is now pursuing her original passion: watercolor painting.

The way my parents lived their lives instilled in me moral integrity and the courage to stand up for what is right not only for myself, but for others that may not be able to stand up for themselves. The integrity was not based in anger, but a combination of grief (deep care and sensitivity for life and others suffering) and joy (justice and empowerment for all). Co-creating an activist business was a combination of passion for pursuing something that I loved and believed in, and doing something with integrity. The integrity keeps our business honest and fresh as we strive to carry products that we believe in and that come from other similar small, local businesses. Over the past eight years we co-created with a handful of other businesses a Northern California network of filling stations and biodiesel producers that just carry biodiesel made from recycled vegetable oil from restaurants.

It's taken a long time, hard work, and even more patience, but we have created jobs for ourselves. I feel so good about the money that I receive from my work, because it is such a clean source of income. Not only is it not coming from petroleum or big corporations, but our customers often give us their money with a smile and from their heart, thanking us for existing and doing what we do. My vision is that big corporations will not have to be overthrown, but will slowly die as more and more people turn away and work for small businesses in the growing local economy.

Slowing down and living simply on less money is how I grew up. My family walked and took public transit all the time. Driving was done sparingly when we really needed to. We had a huge vegetable garden and compost bin. We canned and froze a lot from the garden to eat during the cold Milwaukee winters. Now living in Oakland, I have chickens for eggs, bees for honey, and a vegetable garden. I work 25–30 hours a week and spend my time growing food and cooking for myself. I spend most of my money locally on food at the farmers market and small restaurants, healthcare at the local community acupuncture clinic, and plant starts at the local nursery. Most of which buy biodiesel from our station, as the money circles back and forth, round and round, creating a new economy, local and full of heart.

About the Editor

Lyle Estill and his family now live in a beautiful, new, passive solar home on the edge of a pond in Moncure, North Carolina. Since moving in he has been suffering from oikomania—a word he learned one night playing Balderdash with friends. It means an "abnormal love of home."

When he is not working at Piedmont Biofuels, or corralling authors for a writing project, he can often be found laying block for retaining walls and terraces, clearing brush or putting up firewood that he trades with his neighbors. He also spends an inordinate amount of time creating garden spaces, despite the fact that most of his agricultural production efforts would be considered "flops."

He continues to give weekly tours of Piedmont Biofuels, and of the "eco-industrial" park which Piedmont anchors. He is actively engaged in Slow Money North Carolina, and he is busy figuring out ways to localize investment portfolios.

He remains an advisor to the Abundance Foundation, which is a non-profit that is focused on renewable energy, local food, and building community. His wife, Tami Schwerin, currently runs Abundance.

After twenty-two years together, Tami remains one of the great fixations of his life...

If you have enjoyed *Small Stories, Big Changes* you might also enjoy other

BOOKS TO BUILD A NEW SOCIETY

Our books provide positive solutions for people who want to make a difference. We specialize in:

Sustainable Living • Green Building • Peak Oil •
Renewable Energy • Environment & Economy Natural
Building & Appropriate Technology • Progressive Leadership
Resistance and Community • Educational & Parenting Resources

New Society Publishers

ENVIRONMENTAL BENEFITS STATEMENT

New Society Publishers has chosen to produce this book on recycled paper made with **100% post consumer waste,** processed chlorine free, and old growth free.

For every 5,000 books printed, New Society saves the following resources:[1]

20	Trees
1,773	Pounds of Solid Waste
1,951	Gallons of Water
2,545	Kilowatt Hours of Electricity
3,223	Pounds of Greenhouse Gases
14	Pounds of HAPs, VOCs, and AOX Combined
5	Cubic Yards of Landfill Space

[1]Environmental benefits are calculated based on research done by the Environmental Defense Fund and other members of the Paper Task Force who study the environmental impacts of the paper industry.

For a full list of NSP's titles, please call 1-800-567-6772 *or visit our website* at:

www.newsociety.com